SWEET PICKLES

27 Adorable Knits
for Babies and Toddlers

ANNA ENGE and HEIDI GRØNVOLD

Martingale®
Create with Confidence

Sweet Pickles: 27 Adorable Knits for Babies and Toddlers
© 2016 by Anna Enge and Heidi Grønvold

Martingale®
19021 120th Ave. NE, Ste. 102
Bothell, WA 98011-9511 USA
ShopMartingale.com

Printed in China
21 20 19 18 17 16   8 7 6 5 4 3 2 1

Library of Congress Cataloging-in-Publication Data is available upon request.

ISBN: 978-1-60468-757-6

MISSION STATEMENT

Dedicated to providing quality products and service to inspire creativity.

CREDITS

PUBLISHER AND CHIEF VISIONARY OFFICER
Jennifer Erbe Keltner

EDITORIAL DIRECTOR
Karen Costello Soltys

MANAGING EDITOR
Tina Cook

ACQUISITIONS EDITOR
Karen M. Burns

TECHNICAL EDITOR
Amy Polcyn

COPY EDITOR
Sheila Chapman Ryan

DESIGN DIRECTOR
Paula Schlosser

PHOTOGRAPHERS
Anna Enge and
Heidi Grønvold

PRODUCTION MANAGER
Regina Girard

**COVER AND
INTERIOR DESIGNER**
Adrienne Smitke

ILLUSTRATOR
Kathryn Conway

Contents

Introduction

We're Anna and Heidi, and together we are Pickles.
Our yarn shop, located in Oslo, Norway, is named Pickles, as is our very own brand of yarn. While we are both trained artists who met while working as art directors at a large advertising agency in our former lives, we now express our artistry in designing knitwear. Like most Norwegians, we learned to knit as children, and our love of the craft has never waned.

Whether designing for women, men, or children, our goal is to create interesting designs, sometimes with a whimsical touch of color play, and always with a minimal amount of finishing work. After all, like you, we enjoy knitting with wonderful yarns and seeing the designs emerge on our knitting needles much more than we like sewing seams, grafting stitches, or weaving in ends!

Our designs have been showcased in magazines and on knitting websites, but this is our first collection of patterns published in English, and we're happy to bring you more than 25 designs for babies and children in the pages of this book. Just as with our adult-sized patterns, we want the garments to be not only fun to knit, but fun for little ones to enjoy wearing.

Some of the designs in this book are clearly for Baby. But the other patterns are given in a wide range of sizes, so whether you're knitting for a toddler or a grade-schooler, you'll be able to knit just the right size for your favorite little Sweet Pickle.

~ Anna & Heidi

Sizes

To fit ages 1–2 (3–5, 6–8) years

PONCHO

Circumference: 31 (34¼, 37¼)" at widest point

Length: 7 (8½, 9¾)", excluding collar

HAT

Circumference: 13 (14, 15¼)"

Materials

Worsted-weight merino wool (100% merino wool; 100 g; 220 yds) in the following amounts and colors:

A: 440 (440, 440) yds in pink

B: 220 (220, 440) yds in gray

US Size 6 (4 mm) 16" and 32" circular and double-pointed needles, or size needed to obtain gauge

Stitch markers, tapestry needle

Magic Poncho with Pom-Pom Hat

This knit duo is fun and easy, and the poncho can also be worn as a skirt.

SKILL LEVEL: Easy

Gauge

18 sts and 30 rows = 4" in St st

26 sts and 30 rows = 4" in rib patt, unstretched

Hat

With circular needle and A, CO 84 (92, 100) sts. Pm and join, being careful not to twist the sts.

Work in K1, P1 rib for 4 (4¾, 4¾)".

Next rnd: Change to St st, inc 4 sts evenly around—88 (96, 104) sts.

With A, knit 5 rnds. With B, purl 1 rnd.

Rep last 6 rnds until there are a total of 5 (6, 7) purl stripes.

Shape Crown

Note: Change to dpns when needed.

Rnds 1–4: With A, knit.

Rnd 5 (dec): With A, knit, dec 20 (22, 24) sts evenly around.

Rnd 6: With B, purl.

Rep last 6 rnds twice more—28 (30, 32) sts.

Next rnd: With A, *K2tog; rep from * around—14 (15, 16) sts.

Cut yarn, draw through rem sts, pull tight, and secure.

Weave in ends. Block.

Pom-Pom

With A, wrap yarn around 2" piece of cardboard (or desired size); tie firmly in center. Cut ends and trim to desired shape. Sew to top of hat. Alternately, use a pom-pom maker, following manufacturer's instructions.

Poncho

With circular needle and A, CO 80 (88, 96) sts. Pm and join, being careful not to twist the sts.

Work in K1, P1 rib for 6¼ (7, 8)".

Knit 1 rnd.

*Next rnd: Change to St st, inc 20 (22, 24) sts evenly around.

With A, purl 1 rnd. With B, knit 13 (15, 19) rnds. Rep from * until there are 3 B stripes—140 (154, 168) sts.

Work in K1, P1 rib for 1½". BO.

Weave in ends. Block.

. . . .

Arrow Sweater

This A-line sweater has a top-down raglan increase, but the increase is made in the center back and front as well as on the top of the shoulder to create the arrow shape and make the construction the main design element of the garment.

SKILL LEVEL: Easy

Gauge

20 sts and 32 rows = 4" in St st

Yoke

With A, loosely CO 60 (60, 64, 68, 72) sts. Knit 6 rows (3 garter ridges).

Pm and join in rnd. Rnd beg at center back.

Next rnd: *K15 (15, 16, 17, 18), pm, rep from * to end (4 markers total).**

Change to B (or next color in sequence: C, D, E, F).

Next (inc) rnd: K1, M1L, *knit to 1 st before marker, M1R, K2, M1L; rep from * to last st, M1R, K1.

Knit 2 rnds. Rep inc rnd.

Knit 1 rnd. Change to A, knit 1 rnd.

Rep from ** a total of 8 (9, 10, 11, 12) times—188 (204, 224, 244, 264) sts. On last A rnd, separate sleeves as follows:

Next rnd: K28 (31, 34, 37, 40), place 38 (40, 44, 48, 52) sts on holder for sleeve, pm to mark side "seam," K56 (62, 68, 74, 80), place 38 (40, 44, 48, 52) sts on holder for sleeve, pm to mark side "seam," K28 (31, 34, 37, 40)—112 (124, 136, 148, 160) body sts. Leave markers on sleeve sts in place.

Sizes

To fit ages 1–2 (3–4, 5–6, 7–8) years

Chest: 19½ (22, 24½, 26, 28¼)"

Length: 13½ (15, 17¼, 19, 20½)"

Materials

DK-weight cotton blend (70% cotton, 30% merino wool; 50 g; 129 yds) in the following amounts and colors: **3**

A: 129 (129, 129, 258, 258) yds in cream

B: 129 (129, 129, 258, 258) yds in green

C: 129 (129, 129, 258, 258) yds in light orange

D: 129 (129, 129, 258, 258) yds in dark orange

E: 129 (129, 129, 258, 258) yds in light blue

F: 129 (129, 129, 258, 258) yds in teal

US Size 4 (3.5 mm) 16" and 32" circular and double-pointed needles, or size needed to obtain gauge

US Size E-4 (3.5 mm) crochet hook

1 button, approx ¾" diameter

Stitch markers, stitch holders, tapestry needle

Body

Read entire instructions before proceeding.

Work stripe patt as follows:

Next (chevron) rnd: With next color in sequence, *K1, M1L, knit to 3 sts before next marker, ssk, K2, K2tog, knit to 1 st before next marker, M1R, K1; rep from * around.

Knit 2 rnds even.

Rep chevron rnd. Knit 1 rnd even.

With A, knit 1 rnd.

Rep last 6 rnds using next patt color each time through, and AT SAME TIME, work every 4th chevron rnd as follows to shape body:

Inc chevron rnd: *K1, M1L, knit to last st before center-front marker, M1R, K1; rep from * to end over rem sts (4 sts inc: 2 on each side of center-front and center-back marker).

Work in patt until there are 6 (7, 9, 10, 11) stripes—124 (136, 152, 168, 180) sts.

With A, work in garter st (knit 1 rnd, purl 1 rnd) for 1½ (1½, 2, 2, 2)". BO.

Sleeves

Place 38 (40, 44, 48, 52) sleeve sts on needles. Pm and join. Rnd beg at underarm. Work in stripe patt until there are 4 (5, 7, 8, 9) stripes, working chevron rnd of patt as follows:

Next (chevron) rnd: *K1, K2tog, knit to 3 sts before marker, M1R, K2, M1L, knit to last 2 sts, ssk.

On last A rnd, dec 4 (4, 6, 6, 6) sts evenly around—34 (36, 38, 42, 46) sts.

Work in garter st for 1 (1, 1½, 1½, 1½)". BO.

Finishing

Sew underarm openings closed. With crochet hook, make ch long enough to fit around button, fasten off. Sew in place on left side of back (at the neck) as a button loop, sew button opposite. Weave in ends. Block.

Cool Kid Capris

These soft capri pants will fit your child for two years—first as pants and next as shorts! The larger sizes have wider legs than the smaller ones.

SKILL LEVEL: Intermediate

Sizes

To fit ages 0–3 months (6, 12, 24 months)

Waist: 18 (19, 19½, 21)"

Length: 10½ (12½, 14½, 16½)"

Materials

DK-weight cotton (100% cotton; 50 g; 98 yds) in the following amounts and colors:

A: 98 (98, 196, 196) yds in gray

B: 98 (98, 196, 196) yds in light blue

C: 98 (98, 196, 196) yds in blue

US Size 7 (4.5 mm) 16" and circular and double-pointed needles, or size needed to obtain gauge

Stitch markers, stitch holders, tapestry needle

Gauge

17 sts = 4" in St st

Special Technique

Wrap and turn: Slip next st to RH needle, bring yarn to front/back (opposite side from previous st), sl st back to LH needle, return yarn to back/front for working next st.

Capri Pants

With circular needle and A, CO 76 (80, 84, 92) sts. Pm and join, being careful not to twist the sts. Place 3 additional markers, each 19 (20, 21, 23) sts apart to mark side "seams" and center front and back. Work in St st for 1¾".

Next (eyelet) rnd: K34 (36, 38, 42), K2tog, YO, K4, K2tog, YO, K34 (36, 38, 42).

Short Rows for Back

Row 1: Work in St st to 5 (6, 6, 7) sts past center-back marker, wrap and turn.

Row 2: Work in St st to 5 (6, 6, 7) sts on opposite side of center-back marker, wrap and turn.

Row 3: Work in St st to 10 (12, 12, 14) sts past center-back marker, wrap and turn.

Row 4: Work in St st to 10 (12, 12, 14) sts on opposite side of center-back marker, wrap and turn.

Row 5: Work in St st to 15 (18, 18, 21) sts past center-back marker, wrap and turn.

Row 6: Work in St st to 15 (18, 18, 21) sts on opposite side of center-back marker, wrap and turn.

Work in the Round

Work in St st on all sts for ½" more. Beg stripe patt as follows:

Rnds 1–5: With B, knit.

Rnds 6–10: With C, knit.

Work in stripe patt until piece measures 6¼ (7, 7½, 7¾)" in the front.

Cont in stripe patt and shape crotch as follows:

Next (inc) rnd: *Knit to 2 sts before center-front marker, M1, K4, M1; rep from * on back (4 sts inc).

Next rnd: Knit.

Rep last 2 rnds a total of 3 (4, 5, 6) times—88 (96, 104, 116) sts.

BO 4 sts at center front and 4 sts at center back—80 (88, 96, 108) sts.

Legs

Place half of rem sts on dpns for first leg—40 (44, 48, 54) sts. Pm and join. Place rem sts on holder for second leg. Work even in stripe patt until piece measures 3½ (4¾, 6, 7½)" from BO. Change to A and work 10 rnds more. BO. Rep for other leg.

Finishing

Sew crotch seam closed.

Drawstring

Work in I-cord (page 109) as follows to approx 20" longer than waist measurement:

With dpns and A, CO 4 sts. Knit across row, do not turn, slide sts to opposite end of dpn, pull gently to tighten.

Rep for patt.

Fold upper edge of waistband to WS and sew in place. Insert I-cord in casing through eyelet openings. Weave in ends. Block.

Cool Kid Hooded Hat

A cute topper that stays on little heads without strings—and with a lot of style. Vary the stripe pattern to achieve a custom look.

SKILL LEVEL: Easy

Gauge

14 sts = 4" in garter st using smaller needle with yarn held double

Hat

Note: Use yarn held double throughout.

With larger needle and A, CO 80 (88, 96, 104) sts. Change to smaller circular needle, pm and join, being careful not to twist the sts. Work in garter st (knit 1 rnd, purl 1 rnd), adding stripes of B as desired, until piece measures 4 (4¼, 4¾, 5)".

Next rnd: *K2tog; rep from * around—40 (44, 48, 52) sts.

Work in K2, P2 rib for 1½ (1½, 2, 2)".

Next rnd: K16 (18, 20, 22) sts in patt, BO next 8 sts, K16 (18, 20, 22) sts in patt. Cut yarn. Leave marker in place at beg of rnd (back of head).

Beg working in rows in garter st (knit every row) as follows:

Row 1: Knit.

Row 2: K2tog, knit to last 2 sts, K2tog (2 sts dec).

Rep last 2 rows a total of 2 (2, 3, 3) times.

AT THE SAME TIME, inc at back of head every other row 8 times as follows:

Knit to 1 st before marker, M1R, K2, M1L, knit to end—44 (48, 50, 54) sts.

Sizes

To fit ages 6–12 months (1–2 years, 3–4 years, 5–6 years)

Circumference: 22¾ (25, 27½, 29¾)" at lower edge

Materials

DK-weight merino wool (100% merino wool; 50 g; 153 yds) in the following amounts and colors: ⬛3

A: 306 (459, 459, 459) yds in gray

B: 153 (153, 153, 153) yds in yellow

US Size 8 (5 mm) 16" and 32" circular needles, or size needed to obtain gauge

US Size 13 (9 mm) 32" circular needle

Stitch markers, stitch holders, tapestry needle

Work even in garter st until piece measures 5 (5½, 5, 5½)" from end of rib patt.

Next (inc) row: K1, M1, knit to last st, M1, K1 (2 sts inc).

Rep inc row every ½" a total of 2 (2, 3, 3) times—48 (52, 56, 60) sts.

Work even in garter st until piece measures 6¼ (6¾, 7, 7½)" from end of rib patt, ending with a WS row.

Finishing

Fold hood in half, RS facing you. Join seam using Kitchener st (page 107).

With B, PU 60 (64, 68, 72) sts around front opening. Work in K2, P2 rib for 1 (1¼, 1¼, 1½)". BO loosely in patt. Weave in ends. Block.

Sizes

TUNIC

To fit ages 1 (2–3, 4–5, 6, 8, 10, 12) years

Chest: 21 (23½, 27, 28¼, 30, 32, 34)"

Length: 15 (17, 18, 19, 20, 22, 24½)"

LEGGINGS

To fit ages 1 (2–3, 4–5, 6, 8) years

Waist: 15½ (16¾, 18¾, 21, 22)"

Length: 18 (21½, 24¾, 26¾, 30)"

Materials

Sport-weight wool blend (70% merino wool, 20% mohair, 10% wool; 50 g; 190 yds) in the following amounts and colors: **2**

A: 570 (760, 950, 1140, 1330, 1520, 1710) yds in brown

B: 190 (190, 190, 190, 190, 190, 190) yds in light mint

C: 190 (190, 190, 190, 190, 190, 190) yds in white

D: 380 (570, 760, 950, 1140, 190, 190) yds in lime

US Size 4 (3.5 mm) 16" and 24" to 32" circular and double-pointed needles, or size needed to obtain gauge

US Size 2½ (3 mm) 16" and 24" to 32" circular and double-pointed needles

Stitch markers, stitch holders, tapestry needle

Circle Tunic and Leggings

A delicate ensemble, this set features a fun pattern to knit in a soft wool blend. Narrow sleeves make the tunic comfy under outer garments. The leggings look best on younger children, so the largest two sizes include instructions for the tunic only.

SKILL LEVEL: Intermediate

Gauge

24 sts and 32 rows = 4" in St st using larger needle

30 sts and 32 rows = 4" in rib patt using larger needle, unstretched

Special Technique

Wrap and turn: Sl next st to RH needle, bring yarn to front/back (opposite side from previous st), sl st back to LH needle, return yarn to back/front.

Tunic

The tunic is knit bottom up, with fold-in edges at the bottom and on the sleeves.

Body

With smaller needle and B, CO 156 (168, 188, 196, 208, 220, 228) sts. Pm and join, being careful not to twist the sts. Work in St st for 1¼ (1¼, 1¾, 1¾, 1¾, 2, 2)". Change to larger needle. Purl 1 rnd for turning ridge.

Knit 11 rnds. Measure from here. Change to A and cont in St st in the rnd.

Pm at beg of rnd and after 78 (84, 94, 98, 104, 110, 114) sts to mark side "seams."

Next (dec) rnd: *K3, K2tog, knit to 5 sts before next marker, ssk, K3; rep from * to end (4 sts dec).

Work dec rnd every 1½ (2, 2, 2¼, 2½, 2½, 2½)" a total of 6 times—132 (144, 164, 172, 184, 196, 204) sts.

Work even in St st until piece measures 10¼ (11¾, 12½, 13½, 14, 15¾, 17¾)".

BO 3 sts on each side of each marker for underarms (total of 6 sts per side)—120 (132, 152, 160, 172, 184, 192) sts. Set aside.

Sleeves

With smaller dpns and B, CO 34 (34, 36, 38, 38, 38, 40) sts. Pm and join, being careful not to twist the sts. Work in St st for 1¼ (1¼, 1¾, 1¾, 1¾, 2, 2)". Change to larger dpns. Purl 1 rnd for turning ridge.

Knit 1 rnd. Change to A. Work in St st for 1¼ (1¼, 1¾, 1¾, 1¾, 2, 2)" more.

Next rnd: Knit, inc 4 (4, 6, 6, 8, 10, 12) sts evenly around—38 (38, 42, 44, 46, 48, 52) sts.

Work in St st, inc every 3 (2¼, 2¼, 1¾, 1½, 1¼, 1¼)" a total of 2 (3, 4, 5, 7, 9, 9) times as follows:

Inc rnd: K1, M1L, knit to 1 st before marker, M1R, K1—42 (44, 50, 54, 60, 66, 70) sts.

Work even in St st until piece measures 7 (8¾, 10¼, 11, 11¾, 12½, 13½)".

BO 3 sts on each side of marker for underarms—36 (38, 44, 48, 54, 60, 64) sts. Set aside.

Yoke

Aligning underarms, knit next rnd across sleeve and body sts to join, pm at beg and end of each set of sleeve sts (4 markers total)—192 (208, 240, 256, 280, 304, 320) sts. Rnd begins on back at start of left sleeve.

**Knit 2 (3, 4, 4, 3, 3, 4) rnds.

Sizes 1 and 2–3 years only:

Next rnd: Knit.

All Other Sizes:

Next (dec) rnd: *K1, K2tog, knit to 3 sts before next marker, ssk, K1; rep from * around (8 sts dec).

All Sizes:

Rep from ** 0 (1, 1, 1, 2, 3, 3) times more—192 (208, 224, 240, 256, 272, 288) sts.

Work all rows of chart once—72 (78, 84, 90, 96, 102, 108) sts.

With D, work in K1 tbl, P1 rib for 1¼ (1¼, 1¼, 1¼, 1½, 1½, 1½)". BO loosely.

Finishing

Fold in body and sleeve edges along turning rnd and sew neatly in place. Weave in ends. Block.

Leggings

With smaller circular needle and D, CO 120 (128, 144, 160, 168) sts. Work in K2, P2 rib for 1", beg and ending row with K1 and ending with a WS row.

Next (eyelet) row: K1, YO, P2tog, *K2, YO, P2tog; rep from * to last st, K1.

Pm and join. Place 3 additional markers, each 30 (32, 36, 40, 42) sts apart to mark side "seams" and center front and back.

Short Rows for Back

Row 1: Work in rib patt to 8 (9, 10, 11, 12) sts past center-back marker, wrap and turn.

Row 2: Work in rib patt to 8 (9, 10, 11, 12) sts on opposite side of center-back marker, wrap and turn.

Row 3: Work in rib patt to 16 (18, 20, 22, 24) sts past center-back marker, wrap and turn.

Row 4: Work in rib patt to 16 (18, 20, 22, 24) sts on opposite side of center-back marker, wrap and turn.

Row 5: Work in rib patt to 24 (27, 30, 33, 36) sts past center-back marker, wrap and turn.

Row 6: Work in rib patt to 24 (27, 30, 33, 36) sts on opposite side of center-back marker, wrap and turn.

Work in the Round

Work even in rib patt until piece measures 7¾ (8½, 9, 9½, 10)".

Next (inc) rnd: *Work in patt to 2 sts before center-front marker, M1, K4, M1; rep from * on back (4 sts inc).

Next rnd: Work in patt, working new sts in St st.

Rep last 2 rnds a total of 5 times—140 (148, 164, 180, 188) sts.

BO 10 sts at center front and 10 sts at center back—120 (128, 144, 160, 168) sts.

Legs

Place half of rem sts on dpns for first leg—60 (64, 72, 80, 84) sts. Pm and join. Place rem sts on holder for second leg. Work even in patt until piece measures 15¾ (19, 22, 23½, 26¾)" in the front.

Next rnd: *K2tog, P2; rep from * around—45 (48, 54, 60, 63) sts.

Work in K1, P2 rib for 2¼ (3, 3, 3, 3)" more. BO loosely. Rep for other leg.

Finishing

Sew crotch seam closed.

Drawstring

Work I-cord (page 109) as follows to approx 20" longer than waist measurement:

With smaller dpns and D, CO 4 sts. Knit across row, do not turn, slide sts to opposite end of dpn, pull gently to tighten.

Rep for patt.

Thread through eyelet rnd.

Weave in ends. Block.

Yoke Chart

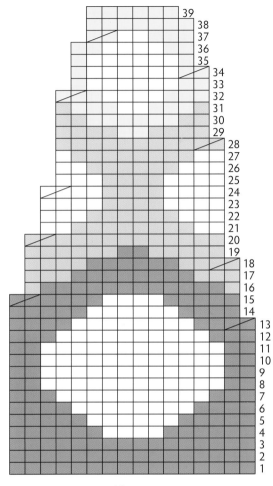

16-st rep

Legend

☐ K on RS, P on WS

◿ K2tog

Sizes

To fit ages 1 (2, 3–4, 5–6, 7–8) years

Chest: 21 (23½, 25, 27, 28¼)"

Length: 13½ (14, 15, 16, 17¼)"

Materials

DK-weight alpaca (100% alpaca; 50 g; 109 yds) in the following amounts and colors: **3**

A: 327 (436, 545, 654, 763) yds in gray

B: 109 yds (all sizes) in pink

C: 109 yds (all sizes) in lime

D: 109 yds (all sizes) in navy

US Size 4 (3.5 mm) 24" to 32" circular and double-pointed needles, or size needed to obtain gauge

US Size 2½ (3 mm) 24" to 32" circular and double-pointed needles

7 buttons, approx ¾" diameter

Stitch markers, stitch holders, tapestry needle

Cute Candy Cardigan

How adorable—a classic cardigan with a colorful touch! Use all the colors in your scrap-yarn basket to make a unique yoke.

SKILL LEVEL: Intermediate

Gauge

19 sts and 28 rows = 4" in St st using larger needle

19 sts and 40 rows = 4" in woven st using larger needle

Yoke

With smaller circular needle and A, CO 49 (55, 61, 67, 67) sts. Knit 4 rows. Change to larger needle.

Next row (RS): K6 (7, 8, 9, 9), pm, K10 (11, 12, 13, 13), pm, K17 (19, 21, 23, 23), pm, K10 (11, 12, 13, 13), pm, knit to end.

Work in woven patt as follows, alternating B, C, and D for contrast color (CC):

Row 1: *Sl 1 wyib; with CC, K1; rep from * to last st, sl 1.

Row 2: *Sl 1 wyif; with CC, K1; rep from * to last st, sl 1.

Rows 3 and 7 (inc row): *With A, knit to 1 st before next marker, M1, K2, M1; rep from * around (8 sts inc).

Rows 4 and 8: With A, knit.

Row 5: *With CC, K1, sl 1 wyib; rep from * to last st, with CC, K1.

Row 6: *With CC, K1; sl 1 wyif; rep from * to last st, with CC, K1.

Rep rows 1–8 a total of 13 (15, 16, 17, 19) times—153 (175, 189, 203, 219) sts. Place each set of 36 (41, 44, 47, 51) sleeve sts on holder.

Body

Cont in St st with A only on 81 (93, 101, 109, 117) body sts.

Next row (RS): Knit to first underarm, and AT THE SAME TIME, inc 2 sts evenly across first front; CO 4 sts at underarm, knit to second underarm, and AT THE SAME TIME, inc 4 sts evenly across back; CO 4 sts at underarm, knit to end, and AT THE SAME TIME, inc 2 sts evenly across second front—97 (109, 117, 125, 133) sts.

Work even in St st until piece measures 12½ (13½, 14, 15¼, 16)".

Next row: With smaller needle, dec 8 (8, 8, 12, 12) sts evenly across—89 (101, 109, 113, 121) sts. Do not BO.

Front Bands

Pm at lower corners. Using same needles, PU 52 (54, 58, 62, 66) sts along each front edge. Work each row across all sts on both sides and lower edge.

Next (inc) row: *Knit to 1 st before marker, M1, K2, M1; rep from * across, knit to end.

Next row: Knit.

Rep last 2 rows for ½". Mark location of 7 buttonholes along 1 band.

Next row: Work in patt as before, working (K2tog, YO) at each buttonhole marker.

Work in patt until band measures approx 1". BO.

Sleeves

Place 36 (41, 44, 47, 51) held sleeve sts on larger dpns. Join yarn and CO 4 sts at underarm. Knit to end of rnd, inc 2 sts evenly—42 (47, 50, 53, 57) sts. Pm to mark beg of rnd.

Work even in St st until piece measures 6¼ (7¾, 9½, 10½, 11¾)".

Next rnd: Dec 16 (19, 20, 23, 25) sts evenly around—26 (28, 30, 30, 32) sts.

Change to smaller dpns. Work in garter st for 1¼". BO.

Finishing

Sew gap under arms. Weave in ends. Block. Sew buttons opposite buttonholes.

Kitty Hat

Bound to be your kid's next favorite, Kitty Hat is fun to knit, fits snugly, and will warm your child's ears. It can be tied under the chin if desired.

SKILL LEVEL: Intermediate

Gauge

18 sts and 28 rows = 4" in St st

Earflaps (Make 2)

Work I-cord (page 109) for 5½ (6, 6¼, 6¾, 7)" as follows:

With dpns, CO 4 sts. Knit across row, do not turn, slide sts to opposite end of dpn, pull gently to tighten.

Rep for patt.

When I-cord is complete, cont earflap as follows:

Row 1 (RS): K1 tbl, K1, M1, K1, sl 1 wyif—5 sts.

Row 2 (WS): K1 tbl, K1, purl to last 2 sts, K1, sl 1 wyif.

Row 3: K1 tbl, K1, M1R, knit to last 2 sts, M1L, K1, sl 1 wyif.

Rep rows 2 and 3 until there are 17 (19, 21, 23, 23) sts. Set aside.

Hat

With circular needle, CO 14 (16, 18, 20, 22) sts for front, knit across first earflap, pm, CO 8 (10, 12, 14, 16) sts for back, knit across second earflap, pm—56 (64, 72, 80, 84) sts.

Next rnd: P14 (16, 18, 20, 22) sts, knit across first earflap, P8 (10, 12, 14, 16) sts, knit across second earflap.

Knit all sts until piece measures 3 (4, 4¾, 5½, 6¼)" from joining rnd.

Sizes

To fit ages 6 months (1 year, 2–3 years, 4–5 years, 6–8 years)

Circumference: 12½ (14¼, 16, 17¾, 18½)"

Materials

220 yds of worsted-weight merino wool (100% merino wool; 100 g; 220 yds) in gray
4

US Size 7 (4.5 mm) 16" circular and double-pointed needles, or size needed to obtain gauge

Stitch markers, stitch holders, tapestry needle

Next (dec) rnd: K1 (0, 1, 0, 2), K2tog 6 (8, 8, 10, 9) times, knit to 2 (3, 2, 3, 1) sts before next marker, K2tog 6 (8, 8, 10, 9) times, knit to end—44 (48, 56, 60, 66) sts.

Work even in St st for 1 (1, 1¼, 1½, 1½)".

Shape Ears

K1 (0, 1, 0, 2) sts past marker at beg of rnd. Working over next 6 (8, 8, 10, 9) sts only, work in St st for 4 rows. Place on holder. Cut yarn, leaving an 8" tail.

Knit next 16 (16, 20, 20, 24) sts onto dpn for first ear and set aside. Join next 6 (8, 8, 10, 9) sts to 6 (8, 8, 10, 9) sts on holder using Kitchener st (page 107). PU 4 sts from inside edge of this center strip for a total of 20 (20, 24, 24, 28) ear sts on dpns. Join. Pm in center of the 4 picked-up sts. Pm 10 (10, 12, 12, 14) sts from first marker to mark opposite side edge. Work in St st

on 20 (20, 24, 24, 28) ear sts for 3 (4, 4, 5, 5) rnds. Rem hat sts are unworked at this time.

Next (dec) rnd: *K2, ssk, knit to 3 sts before marker, K2tog, K1; rep from * around (4 sts dec).

Next rnd: Knit.

Rep last 2 rnds a total of 3 (3, 4, 4, 5) times—8 (8, 8, 8, 8) sts.

Next rnd: *Ssk, K2tog; rep from * around—4 (4, 4, 4, 4) sts. Join rem sts at tip of ear using Kitchener st.

Make second ear as for first, using rem sts.

Finishing

Weave in ends. Block.

• • • • • • • • • • • •

Sizes

To fit ages 6–12 months (1 year, 2–3 years, 4–5 years, 6–7 years, 8–9 years, 10–12 years)

Chest: 19 (21, 23, 25, 27, 29, 32)"

Length: 10½ (11½", 14, 15½, 17, 19, 21)"

Materials

375 (500, 500, 625, 750, 875, 1000) yds of DK-weight angora blend (70% angora, 20% nylon, 10% wool; 25 g; 125 yds) in lime

OR

459 (612, 612, 765, 918, 1071, 1224) yds of DK-weight merino wool (100% merino wool; 50 g; 153 yds) in gray

US Size 4 (3.5 mm) 32" circular and double-pointed needles, or size needed to obtain gauge

US Size 3 (3.25 mm) 32" circular and double-pointed needles

5 to 10 buttons, approx ¾" diameter

Stitch markers, stitch holders, tapestry needle

Hooded Garter Cardigan

Hoods are always popular, and this hooded cardigan is both easy and warm. Babies and big kids alike will love wearing this hoodie.

SKILL LEVEL: Easy

Gauge

20 sts and 40 rows = 4" in garter st using larger needle

Working Buttonholes

Slip first st of each row throughout. Buttonholes should be started after 2 garter ridges (4 rows) and worked approx every 2" thereafter as follows:

Girls buttonhole row (RS): K2, YO, K2tog, knit to end.

Boys buttonhole row (RS): Knit to last 3 sts, YO, K2tog, K1.

Body

With smaller circular needle, CO 100 (108, 120, 128, 136, 152, 164) sts. Work in garter st (knit every row) for 1 (1, 1¼, 1¼, 1¼, 1½, 1½)". Change to larger needle and cont in garter st until piece measures 6½ (7, 9, 10½, 11½, 13, 14½)", ending with a RS row—26 (28, 31, 33, 35, 39, 42) sts for right and left fronts; 48 (52, 58, 62, 66, 74, 80) sts in center of row for back.

Left Front

Work in garter st over first 26 (28, 31, 33, 35, 39, 42) sts *only* for 4 (4¼, 4¾, 5¼, 5½, 6, 6½)" more. Place on holder.

Back

Join yarn and work in garter st over center 48 (52, 58, 62, 66, 74, 80) sts until back measures same as left front. Place on holder.

Right Front

Work as for left front over rem 26 (28, 31, 33, 35, 39, 42) sts.

Join shoulders using Kitchener st (page 107) for 11 (12, 14, 15, 16, 19, 21) sts on each side, counting from side edge. Leave rem 56 (60, 64, 68, 72, 76, 80) sts on hold for hood.

Hood

Pm in center back of rem 56 (60 64, 68, 72, 76, 80) hood sts. Knit 3 rows, ending with a WS row.

Next (inc) row (RS): Knit to 1 st before marker, M1, knit to 1 st after marker, M1, knit to end (2 sts inc).

Next row: Knit.

Rep last 2 rows 12 times—80 (84, 88, 92, 96, 100, 104) sts.

Work even in garter st until hood measures 6½ (7, 7¼, 7¼, 7½, 7½, 8)" past first inc. Fold hood in half, join top seam using Kitchener st.

Sleeves

With larger needle and RS facing you, PU 40 (44, 48, 52, 60, 64) sts around armhole opening. Pm and join. Beg with a purl rnd, work in garter st (knit 1 rnd, purl 1 rnd) for 1½", ending with a purl rnd.

Next (dec) rnd: K1, K2tog, knit to last 3 sts, K2tog, knit to end (2 sts dec).

Rep dec round every 1½" another 3 (4, 5, 6, 7, 8, 9) times more—32 (34, 36, 38, 40, 42, 44) sts.

Work even until sleeve measures 6 (6½, 8½, 9½, 10½, 12, 14)". Change to smaller needles. Work in garter st for 1½" more. BO loosely.

Finishing

Weave in ends. Block. Sew buttons opposite buttonholes.

• • • • • • • • • • •

Garland Sweater with Stripy Pants

A classic sweater with stripy pants, this set's colorwork just makes you happy. The pants are knit with the leftover sweater yarn, so feel free to indulge in colors! The pants look best on younger children, so the largest two sizes include instructions for the sweater only.

SKILL LEVEL: Intermediate

Gauge

18 sts and 26 rows = 4" in St st with yarn held double using larger needle

24 sts and 26 rows = 4" in rib patt with yarn held double using larger needle, unstretched

Special Technique

Wrap and turn: Sl next st to RH needle, bring yarn to front/back (opposite side from previous st), sl st back to LH needle, return yarn to back/front.

Sweater

This sweater is knit from the bottom up using a double strand of yarn held tog.

Body

With smaller circular needle and A, CO 102 (114, 120, 128, 136, 142, 148) sts. Pm and join, being careful not to twist the sts. Work in K1 tbl, P1 rib for 1¼ (1 14, 1¼, 1½, 1½, 1½, 1½)".

Change to larger needles. Working in St st, inc 10 (10, 12, 12, 12, 14, 16)

Sizes

SWEATER

To fit ages 1 (2–3, 4–5, 6, 8, 10, 12) years

Chest: 24½ (27, 29, 31, 32¼, 34, 35½)"

Length: 14½ (16½, 17¾, 18½, 19¾, 20½, 22)"

PANTS

To fit ages 1 (2–3, 4–5, 6, 8) years

Waist: 15 (15½, 16½, 18, 19½)"

Length: 18 (22¾, 26, 27½, 30)"

Materials

Sport-weight alpaca (100% alpaca; 50 g; 209 yds) (2) as follows:

A: 836 (1045, 1254, 1463, 1463, 1672, 1881) yds in gray

B: 209 yds (all sizes) in yellow

C: 209 yds (all sizes) in dark gray

D: 209 yds (all sizes) in orange

E: 209 yds (all sizes) in navy

F: 209 yds (all sizes) in teal

G: 209 yds (all sizes) in green

H: 209 yds (all sizes) in brown

Note: For pants only, a total of 627 (836, 1045, 1254, 1463) yds in desired colors is required.

Continued on page 34

Continued from page 33

US Size 6 (4 mm) 16" and 24" to 32" circular and double-pointed needles, or size needed to obtain gauge

US Size 4 (3.5 mm) 16" and 24" to 32" circular and double-pointed needles

Stitch markers, stitch holders, tapestry needle

sts evenly on first rnd—112 (124, 132, 140, 148, 156, 164) sts.

Pm 56 (62, 66, 70, 74, 78, 82) sts from first marker to mark opposite side "seam." Work even in St st until piece measures 8¾ (10½, 11½, 12¼, 13, 13¾, 15)".

BO 2 sts each side of each marker for underarms (4 total per side)—104 (116, 124, 132, 140, 148, 156) sts. Set aside.

Sleeves

With smaller dpns and A, loosely CO 28 (30, 30, 32, 32, 32, 34) sts. Pm and join, being careful not to twist the sts. Work in K1 tbl, P1 rib for 1¼ (1¼, 1¼, 1½, 1½, 1½, 1½)".

Change to larger circular needle. Working in St st, inc 4 (6, 6, 6, 8, 8, 8) sts evenly on first rnd—32 (36, 36, 38, 40, 40, 42) sts.

Next (inc) rnd: K1, M1, knit to last st, M1, K1 (2 sts inc).

Rep inc rnd every 1½" a total of 4 (5, 6, 6, 6, 7, 7) times—40 (46, 48, 50, 52, 54, 56) sts.

Work even until piece measures 8¾ (10¼, 11½, 12¼, 13, 13¾, 15)". Bind off 2 sts at beg and end of rnd (4 sts total) —36 (42, 44, 46, 48, 50, 52) sts.

Yoke

Aligning underarms, knit next rnd across sleeve and body sts to join, pm at beg and end of each set of sleeve sts (4 markers total)—176 (200, 212, 224, 236, 248, 260) sts. Rnd begins on back at start of left sleeve.

Next (dec) rnd: K2tog, *knit to 2 sts before next marker, ssk, K2tog; rep from * to last 2 sts, ssk—168 (192, 204, 216, 228, 240, 252) sts.

Work even in St st for ½ (¾, 1¼, 1¼, 1½, 1½, 2)". Beg garland patt following chart, being careful not to strand yarn too tightly—56 (64, 68, 72, 76, 80, 84) sts rem when complete.

Next rnd: With A, knit.

Change to smaller dpns. Work in K1 tbl, P1 rib for 1¼ (1¼, 1¼, 1½, 1½, 1½, 1½)". BO loosely.

Finishing

Sew gap under arms. Weave in ends. Block.

Pants

With smaller circular needle and A, CO 88 (96, 104, 112, 120) sts. Pm and join, being careful not to twist the sts.

Next rnd: K1, *P2, K2; rep from * to last st, K1.

Rep last rnd until piece measures ¾".

Next (eyelet) rnd: K1, YO, P2tog, *K2, YO, P2tog; rep from * to last st, K1.

Work in rib patt as before until piece measures 1½". Change to larger circular needle.

Place 3 more markers, each 22 (24, 26, 28, 30) sts apart to mark side "seams" and center front and back.

Short Rows for Back

Row 1: Work in rib patt to 6 (7, 8, 9, 9) sts past center-back marker, wrap and turn.

Row 2: Work in rib patt to 6 (7, 8, 9, 9) sts on opposite side of center-back marker, wrap and turn.

Row 3: Work in rib patt to 12 (14, 16, 18, 18) sts past center-back marker, wrap and turn.

Row 4: Work in rib patt to 12 (14, 16, 18, 18) sts on opposite side of center-back marker, wrap and turn.

Row 5: Work in rib patt to 18 (21, 24, 27, 27) sts past center-back marker, wrap and turn.

Row 6: Work in rib patt to 18 (21, 24, 27, 27) sts on opposite side of center-back marker, wrap and turn.

Work in the Round

Beg stripe patt by changing colors as desired every 1½". Work in stripe patt until piece measures 7¾ (9, 9½, 9¾, 10¼)" in the front.

Cont in stripe and rib patt and shape crotch as follows:

Next (inc) rnd: *Work in patt to 2 sts before center-front marker, M1, K4, M1; rep from * on back (4 sts inc).

Next rnd: Work even in patt.

Rep last 2 rnds a total of 3 times—100 (108, 116, 124, 132) sts.

BO 6 sts at center front and 6 sts at center back—88 (96, 104, 112, 120) sts.

Legs

Place half of rem sts on dpns for first leg—44 (48, 52, 56, 60) sts. Pm and join. Place rem sts on holder for second leg. Work even in stripe patt until piece measures 15¾ (19¾, 22¾, 24½, 26¾)" in front. Change to smaller dpns.

Next (turning) rnd: *K2tog, P2; rep from * around—33 (36, 39, 42, 45) sts.

Work even in K1, P2 rib for 2½ (3, 3, 3, 3)". BO. Rep for other leg.

Finishing

Sew crotch seam closed. Fold cuffs along turning rnd and sew in place.

Drawstring

Work I-cord (page 109) to approx 20" longer than waist measurement as follows:

With dpns and A, CO 4 sts. Knit across row, do not turn, slide sts to opposite end of dpn, pull gently to tighten.

Rep for patt.

Thread through eyelet rnd.

Weave in ends. Block.

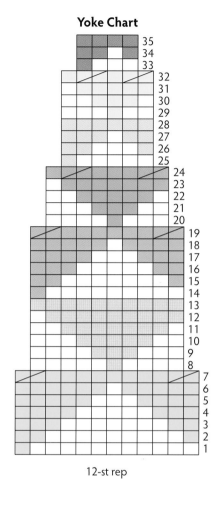

Yoke Chart

12-st rep

Legend

☐ K

◩ K2tog

Sizes

To fit ages 0–3 months (6–12 months, 1 year, 2 years, 3–4 years)

Chest: 21 (23½, 26, 28½, 31)"

Length: 20½ (24½, 27, 30¼, 33½)"

Materials

Sport-weight wool (100% wool; 100 g; 415 yds) in the following amounts and colors: 🔵

A: 415 (415, 415, 415, 830) yds in purple

B: 415 (415, 415, 415, 415) yds in yellow

C: 415 (415, 415, 415, 415) yds in pink

D: 415 (415, 415, 415, 415) yds in lime

E: 415 (415, 415, 415, 415) yds in teal

US Size 8 (5 mm) 16" and 32" circular and double-pointed needles, or size needed to obtain gauge

5 (6, 6, 7, 7) buttons, approx ¾" diameter

Stitch markers, stitch holders, tapestry needle

Rainbow Jumpsuit

A jaunty jumpsuit for your little one is knit in a rainbow of cheery colors. Top-down construction makes matching stripes a breeze.

SKILL LEVEL: Easy

Gauge

16 sts and 24 rows = 4" in St st with yarn held double

24 sts and 24 rows = 4" in rib patt with yarn held double, unstretched

Yoke

Note: Work in stripe patt throughout, alternating colors every ¾" in sequence A, B, C, D, E or as desired. Hold yarn double throughout.

With longest circular needle and A, CO 42 (46, 50, 54, 54) sts. Work in K2, P2 rib, ending with K2, for 1½ (1½, 2, 2, 2)", ending with a RS row. Change to St st.

Next row (WS): P7 (8, 9, 10, 10) for front, pm, P4 for sleeve, pm, P20 (22, 24, 26, 26) for back, pm, P4 for sleeve, pm, purl to end for second front.

Next (inc) row (RS): *Knit to 1 st before next marker, M1L, K2, M1R; rep from * across—8 sts inc.

Next row: Purl.

Rep last 2 rows a total of 9 (11, 13, 14, 16) times—114 (134, 154, 166, 182) sts.

Next (inc) row (RS): *Knit to 1 st after first marker, M1R, knit to 1 st before next marker, M1L; rep from * with rem 2 markers—4 sts inc.

Next row: Purl.

Rep last 2 rows a total of 3 times—126 (146, 166, 178, 194) sts.

Body

Next row (RS): Knit, placing 28 (32, 36, 38, 42) sleeve sts on holders and CO 4 sts at each underarm—78 (90, 102, 110, 118) sts for body.

Work even in St st and stripe patt until piece measures 9½ (12, 12¾, 14¼, 15¾)" from start of yoke shaping. Join with circular needle, CO 6 sts at center front where rnd is joined and pm in center of these 6 sts—84 (96, 108, 116, 124) sts. Pm 42 (48, 54, 58, 62) sts from first marker to mark center back. Rnds beg at center front.

Shape Crotch

Next (inc) rnd: Knit to 3 sts before center-back marker, M1R, K6, M1L, knit to end (2 sts inc).

Next rnd: Knit.

Rep last 2 rnds a total of 4 times—92 (104, 116, 124, 132) sts.

Next (inc) rnd: K3, M1R, knit to 3 sts before center-back marker, M1R, K6, M1L, knit to last 3 sts, M1L, K3—4 sts inc.

Next rnd: Knit.

Rep last 2 rnds a total of 3 times—104 (116, 128, 136, 144) sts.

Knit 1 rnd.

BO 6 sts at center front and 6 sts at center back—92 (104, 116, 124, 132) sts.

Legs

Place half of rem sts on dpns for first leg—46 (52, 58, 62, 66) sts. Pm and join. Place rem sts on holder for second leg.

Next (dec) rnd: K1, K2tog, knit to last 3 sts, ssk, K1—2 sts dec.

Rep dec rnd every 1¼" a total of 6 (7, 9, 10, 11) sts—34 (38, 40, 42, 44) sts.

Work even in patt until piece measures 7 (8½, 10½, 11¾, 13¼)" from BO.

Next rnd: Knit, dec 14 (14, 12, 10, 12) sts evenly around—20 (24, 28, 32, 32) sts.

Work in K2, P2 rib for 1½ (1½, 2, 2, 2)" more. BO loosely. Rep for other leg.

Sleeves

Place 28 (32, 36, 38, 42) held sleeve sts on dpns. CO 4 sts at underarm, pm in center of these 4 sts—32 (36, 40, 42, 46) sts.

Next (dec) rnd: K1, K2tog, knit to last 3 sts, ssk, K1—2 sts dec.

Working in St st and stripe patt, rep dec rnd every 1½" a total of 2 (3, 4, 5, 6) times—28 (30, 32, 32, 34) sts.

Work even until piece measures 4¼ (5½, 6¾, 8, 10)".

Next rnd: Knit, dec 8 (6, 4, 4, 6) sts evenly around—20 (24, 28, 28, 28) sts.

Work in K2, P2 rib for 1½ (1½, 2, 2, 2)". BO.

Finishing

Sew crotch seam closed. Sew gap under arms.

Finish front bands as follows:

With A, PU 20 sts every 4" along left side of center front for button band (or side desired). Work in K2, P2 rib for 1¼". BO.

On opposite side, PU same number of sts and work in K2, P2 rib for ½". Mark location of 5 (6, 6, 7, 7) buttonholes, evenly spaced.

Next row: *Work in patt to marker, P2tog (or K2tog, as appropriate), YO; rep from * across, work in patt to end.

Work even in patt until band measures 1¼". BO.

Lap buttonhole band over button band and sew lower edges tog. Weave in ends. Block. Sew buttons opposite buttonholes.

Everyday Cardigan

Look no further for a good-looking, practical, and warm cardigan for your little one. The striping makes mottled-colored yarns shine.

SKILL LEVEL: Easy

Gauge

18 sts and 26 rows = 4" in St st using larger needle

22 sts and 30 rows = 4" in rib patt using larger needle, unstretched

Body

With smaller circular needle and A, CO 96 (104, 112, 120, 128, 136, 144) sts. Work in K1, P1 rib for ½". Change to larger needles and work in St st, changing colors every 8 rows for stripe patt, until piece measures 9 (10½, 11½, 12½, 13½, 15, 16½)", ending with a WS row.

Next row (RS): K20 (22, 24, 26, 28, 30, 32), BO 4 sts for underarm, K48 (52, 56, 60, 64, 68, 72), BO 4 sts for underarm, knit to end—88 (96, 104, 112, 120, 128, 136) sts.

Sleeves

Note: To match stripes, read ahead and check sleeve length. Compare to body length to determine which color to start with so stripes will align.

With smaller dpns and desired color, CO 28 (32, 34, 36, 38, 38, 40) sts. Work in K1, P1 rib for 1½ (1½, 1½, 2, 2, 2¼, 2¼)". Change to larger needles and St st, working stripe patt as before.

Sizes

To fit ages 1 (2–3, 4–5, 6–7, 8–9, 10–12, 14–16) years

Chest: 23 (24, 26, 28, 30, 32, 33)"

Length: 14 (15½, 17, 18, 19½, 21, 23)"

Materials

Worsted-weight merino wool (100% merino wool; 100 g; 220 yds) in the following amounts and colors: [4]

A: 220 (440, 440, 440, 660, 660, 660) yds in green

B: 220 (440, 440, 440, 660, 660, 660) yds in light blue

US Size 7 (4.5 mm) 32" circular and double-pointed needles, or size needed to obtain gauge

US Size 6 (4 mm) 32" circular and double-pointed needles

7 (8, 8, 9, 10, 10, 11) buttons, approx ¾" diameter

Stitch markers, stitch holders, tapestry needle

Next (inc) rnd: K1, M1R, knit to last st, M1L, K1—2 sts inc.

Rep inc rnd every 1 (1¼, 1½, 1½, 1¾, 1¾, 1¾)" a total of 6 (6, 7, 7, 7, 9, 10) times—40 (44, 48, 50, 52, 56, 60) sts.

Work even until piece measures 8 (9½, 11, 12¼, 13½, 15, 16½)", taking care to end on same point in stripe patt as underarm BO on body. BO 2 sts at beg and end of rnd (4 sts total) for underarm—36 (40, 44, 46, 48, 52, 56) sts.

Yoke

Aligning underarms, knit next row across sleeve and body sts to join, pm at beg and end of each set of sleeve sts (4 markers total)—160 (176, 192, 204, 216, 232, 248) sts.

Purl 1 row.

Next (dec) row (RS): *Knit to 3 sts before marker, ssk, K2, K2tog; rep from * to end—8 sts dec.

Next row: Purl.

Rep last 2 rows a total of 15 (16, 17, 18, 19, 20, 21) times—40 (48, 56, 60, 64, 72, 80) sts. Change to smaller needles. Work in K1, P1 rib for 3 (3, 3½, 3½, 3½, 4, 4)". BO.

Finishing

Sew gap under arms.

Finish front bands as follows:

With smaller needle and B, PU 22 sts every 4" along right side of center front for button band (or size desired). Work in K1, P1 rib for 2½ (2½, 2½, 3, 3, 3½, 3½)". BO.

On opposite side, PU same number of sts and work in K1, P1 rib for 1½". Mark location of 7 (8, 8, 9, 10, 10, 11) buttonholes, evenly spaced.

Next row: *Work in patt to marker, K2tog, YO; rep from * across, work in patt to end.

Work even in patt until band measures 2½ (2½, 2½, 3, 3, 3½, 3½)". BO.

Weave in ends. Block. Sew buttons opposite buttonholes.

· · · · · · · · · ·

Sizes

To fit ages 0–3 (3–6, 9–12) months

CARDIGAN

Chest: 16½ (19, 21)"

Length: 9¾ (13, 15)"

OVERALLS

Width at narrowest point: 7 (8¾, 9½)"

Length: Approx 17 (22½, 27¼)"

Materials

Fingering-weight merino wool (100% merino wool; 100 g; 420 yds) in the following amounts and colors:

A: 420 yds (all sizes) in gray

B: 420 yds (all sizes) in orange

C: 420 yds (all sizes) in blue

D: 420 yds (all sizes) in navy

US Size 5 (3.75 mm) 16" and 32" circular and double-pointed needles, or size needed to obtain gauge

US Size E-4 (3.5 mm) crochet hook

9 buttons, approx ¾" diameter

Stitch markers, stitch holders, tapestry needle

Overalls and Cardigan for Liv

This soft and fun baby set starts with overalls that are topped by a woven-stitch cardigan. The overalls are narrow around the chest and wide around the bum, allowing plenty of room for diapers.

SKILL LEVEL: Intermediate

Gauge

23 sts = 4" in St st

Cardigan

Cardigan is worked top down in 1 piece.

Yoke

With circular needle and A, CO 49 (55, 59) sts. Knit 4 rows.

Next row (RS): K6 (7, 7), pm, K10 (11, 13), pm, K17 (19, 19), pm, K10 (11, 13), pm, knit to end.

Work in woven patt as follows, alternating B, C, D for contrast color (CC):

Row 1: *Sl 1 wyib; with CC, K1; rep from * to last st, sl 1.

Row 2: *Sl 1 wyif; with CC, K1; rep from * to last st, sl 1.

Rows 3 and 7 (inc row): *With A, knit to 1 st before next marker, M1, K2, M1; rep from * around—8 sts inc.

Rows 4 and 8: With A, knit.

Row 5: *With CC, K1, sl 1 wyib; rep from * to last st; with CC, K1.

Row 6: *With CC, K1; sl 1 wyif; rep from * to last st; with CC, K1.

Rep rows 1–8 a total of 12 (14, 17) times—145 (167, 195) sts. Place each set of 34 (39, 47) sleeve sts on holder.

Body

Cont in St st with A only.

Next row (RS): Knit to first underarm, and AT THE SAME TIME, inc 2 (3, 4) sts evenly across first front; CO 2 sts at underarm, knit to second underarm, and AT THE SAME TIME, inc 4 (5, 6) sts evenly across back; CO 2 sts at underarm, knit to end, and AT THE SAME TIME, inc 2 sts evenly across second front—89 (104, 119) sts.

Work even in St st until piece measures 9 (12¼, 14¼)". Do not BO.

Front Bands

Pm at lower corners. Using same needles, PU 40 (52, 62) sts along each front edge. Work each row across all sts on both sides and lower edge.

Next (inc) row: *Knit to 1 st before marker, M1, K2, M1; rep from * across, knit to end.

Next row: Knit.

Rep last 2 rows for ½". Mark location of 7 buttonholes along 1 band.

Next row: Work in patt as before, working (K2tog, YO) at each buttonhole marker.

Work in patt until band measures approx ¾". BO.

Sleeves

Place 34 (39, 47) held sleeve sts on dpns. Join A and CO 2 sts at underarm, pm in center of these 2 sts. Knit to end of rnd—36 (41, 49) sts.

Next (dec) rnd: K1, ssk, knit to last 3 sts, K2tog, K1—2 sts dec.

Rep dec rnd every 1¼" a total of 3 (4, 5) times—30 (33, 39) sts. Work even until piece measures 4 (5½, 6¼)". Work in garter st (knit 1 rnd, purl 1 rnd) for ¾". BO.

Finishing

Sew gap under arms. Weave in ends. Block. Sew buttons opposite buttonholes.

Overalls

Overalls are worked from the cuffs up.

Legs

With dpns and B, CO 34 (36, 40) sts. Pm and join, being careful not to twist the sts. Knit 6 rnds.

Next (turning) rnd: Purl.

Working in St st, alternate B and C every 6 rnds.

Next (inc) rnd: K1, M1R, knit to last st, M1L, K1 (2 sts inc).

Rep inc rnd every ¾" a total of 6 (8, 10) times—46 (52, 60) sts. Work even until piece measures 4¾ (6¼, 8)".

Rep inc rnd every other rnd 3 (4, 4) times—52 (60, 68) sts. Set aside. Rep for other leg.

Body

Place sts from both legs on circular needle, pm at center back, CO 4 sts at center front and center back between legs—112 (128, 144) sts. Change to B, discontinue stripe patt.

Place 3 additional markers, each 28 (32, 36) sts apart to mark side "seams" and center front and back. Work even in St st until piece measures 8½ (13½, 15¾)".

Next (dec) rnd: *Knit to 2 sts before first side marker, ssk, K2tog; rep from * at opposite side marker—4 sts dec.

Rep dec rnd every ¾" a total of 3 (5, 6) times—100 (108, 120) sts. Work even until piece measures 12½ (16½, 19¾)". Change to garter st. Work even for approx ½ (¾, 1¼)" more.

Next rnd: Work in patt, dec 4 sts evenly on front and 4 sts evenly on back—92 (100, 112) sts.

Work even in garter st for 2 rnds. BO 2 sts each side of each side edge marker for underarms (4 sts total per side). Place 42 (46, 52) front sts on holder.

Back

Work in garter st (knit every row) on 42 (46, 52) back sts.

Next (dec) row: K2tog, knit to end (1 st dec).

Next row: Rep dec row—40 (44, 50) sts.

Work even for ¾ (1¼, 1½)". BO center 6 (6, 8) sts, with rem 17 (19, 21) sts each side for shoulder straps.

Straps

Work even in garter st for 1".

Next (dec) row: K2tog, knit to end (1 st dec).

Next row: Rep dec row.

Work even until piece measures 5½ (6, 6¼)". K2tog at beg of each row until 6 (8, 10) sts rem. Work second strap same as first. BO.

Front

Work as for back until straps measure ¾".

Next (buttonhole) row: K7 (8, 9), BO 3 sts, K7 (8, 9).

Next row: Knit, CO 3 sts over gap to close buttonhole.

Work even for ½". K2tog at beg of each row 4 times. Work second strap same as first. BO.

Finishing

Sew crotch seam closed. Fold legs along turning rnd and sew in place. With crochet hook and B, work in single crochet along edges of straps. Fasten off. Weave in ends. Block. Sew buttons opposite buttonholes.

· · · · · · · · ·

Plain Cardigan

A simple cardigan with a charming garter-stitch yoke offers season-spanning appeal.

SKILL LEVEL: Easy

Sizes

To fit ages 0–3 months (6–12 months, 1–2 years, 3–4 years, 5–6 years, 7–8 years)

Chest: 17 (19, 21, 24, 26, 28)"

Length: 9½ (11, 12½, 15½, 17, 18½)"

Materials

218 (436, 436, 654, 654, 654) yds of worsted-weight merino wool (100% merino wool; 100 g; 218 yds) in green [4]

US size 9 (5.5 mm) 32" circular and double-pointed needles, or size needed to obtain gauge

5 to 10 buttons, approx ¾" diameter

Stitch markers, stitch holders, tapestry needle

Gauge

14 sts and 21 rows = 4" in St st

Body

Note: Sl first st of each row throughout. Buttonholes are worked on RS rows every 8 to 10 rows as follows: Sl 1, K1, YO, K2tog, knit to end.

With circular needle, CO 64 (72, 80, 88, 96, 104) sts. Work in garter st for 8 (8, 8, 10, 10, 12) rows. Change to St st, keeping first and last 5 sts in garter st and working buttonholes as described above throughout.

Work even until piece measures 6½ (7½, 8½, 10, 11, 12½)", ending with a WS row.

Next row (RS): K15 (17, 19, 21, 23, 25), BO 4 sts for underarm, K26 (30, 34, 38, 42, 46), BO 4 sts for underarm, K15 (17, 19, 21, 23, 25). Set aside.

Sleeves

With dpns, CO 16 (18, 22, 24, 24, 26) sts. Pm and join, being careful not to twist the sts. Work in garter st for 8 (8, 8, 10, 10, 12) rnds. Change to St st, inc 4 sts evenly on first rnd—20 (22, 26, 28, 28, 30) sts.

*Work even for 2 (2½, 2½, 3, 2½, 3)".

Next (inc) rnd: K1, M1R, knit to last st, M1L, K1—2 sts inc.

Rep from * 2 (2, 2, 2, 3, 3) times total—24 (26, 30, 32, 34, 36) sts.

Work even until piece measures 6½ (7½, 9, 10½, 11½, 14)". Bind off 2 sts each side of marker (4 sts total) for underarm—20 (22, 26, 28, 30, 32) sts.

Yoke

Aligning underarms, knit next row across sleeve and body sts to join, pm at beg and end of each set of sleeve sts (4 markers total)—96 (108, 124, 136, 148, 160) sts.

Knit 1 row.

Next (dec) row (RS): *Knit to 3 sts before marker, ssk, K2, K2tog; rep from * to end—8 sts dec.

Next row: Knit.

Rep last 2 rows a total of 8 (9, 10, 12, 13, 14) times—32 (36, 44, 40, 44, 48) sts. Knit 2 more rows, work final buttonhole. BO.

Finishing

Sew gap under arms. Weave in ends. Block. Sew buttons opposite buttonholes.

· · · · · · · · · · ·

Plain Tunic

Your little one will look adorable! This tunic has an A-line shape, and the buttons can be worn in the front or in the back. It's a favorite all year round.

SKILL LEVEL: Easy

Sizes

To fit ages 1 (2–3, 4–5, 6–7, 8–9) years

Chest: 20½ (22, 23½, 26, 28)"

Length: 16½ (17¼, 20½, 22½, 24½)"

Materials

294 (392, 490, 588, 686) yds of DK-weight cotton (100% cotton; 50 g; 98 yds) in beige **3**

420 (420, 840, 840, 840) yds of fingering-weight merino wool (100% merino; 100 g; 420 yds) in beige **1**

US Size 9 (5.5 mm) 24" and 32" circular needles, or size needed to obtain gauge

US Size G-6 (4 mm) crochet hook

3 buttons, approx ¾" diameter

Stitch markers, stitch holders, tapestry needle

Gauge

14 sts and 21 rows = 4" in St st with 1 strand of each yarn held tog

Body

Note: Hold 1 strand of each yarn tog throughout.

With circular needle, CO 120 (128, 136, 144, 160) sts. Pm and join, being careful not to twist the sts.

Next rnd: K15 (16, 17, 18, 20), pm, [K30 (32, 34, 36, 40), pm] 3 times, K15 (16, 17, 18, 20). Rnds beg at center back.

Work in garter st (knit 1 rnd, purl 1 rnd) until piece measures 1½ (3, 3, 3, 3)". Change to St st.

Next (dec) rnd: K15 (16, 17, 18, 20), sl marker, K2tog, knit to 2 sts before next marker, ssk, work to next marker, sl marker, K2tog, knit to 2 sts before next marker, ssk, knit to end (4 sts dec).

Rep dec rnd every 1" a total of 12 (12, 13, 14, 16) times—72 (80, 84, 88, 96) sts. Work even until piece measures 13¼ (14, 15, 16, 18)".

Next rnd: Knit, BO 6 (8, 8, 8, 8) sts between each pair of side markers—60 (64, 68, 72, 80) sts.

Next rnd: Knit, CO 18 (20, 24, 28, 30) sts over each gap for sleeves—96 (104, 116, 128, 140) sts.

Yoke

Work in garter st in rows from this point forward.

Next (dec) row: Knit, dec 16 (16, 20, 20, 22) sts evenly across—80 (88, 96, 108, 118) sts.

Knit 3 (3, 7, 9, 9) rows.

Next (dec) row: Knit, dec 12 (12, 14, 16, 20) sts evenly across—68 (76, 82, 92, 98) sts.

Knit 3 (3, 7, 9, 9) rows.

Next (dec) row: Knit, dec 12 (12, 12, 14, 18) sts evenly across—56 (64, 70, 78, 80) sts.

Knit 3 (3, 7, 9, 9) rows.

Next (dec) row: Knit, dec 8 (10, 12, 14, 14) sts evenly across—48 (54, 58, 64, 66) sts.

Knit 2 (2, 2, 2, 2) rows. BO loosely.

Finishing

With crochet hook, work in single crochet around neck opening, making 3 ch loops for buttons, evenly spaced along 1 side. Fasten off.

Weave in ends. Block. Sew buttons opposite button loops.

Springtime Vest

Perfect for spring and summer, this quick-and-easy knit vest is made with a skin-friendly mix of organic, plant-dyed cotton and super soft merino.

SKILL LEVEL: Easy

Sizes

To fit ages 1 (2, 3–4, 5–6, 7–8) years

Chest: 22 (24, 25, 27, 29)"

Length: 11¼ (11¾, 15, 17½, 20)"

Materials

252 (378, 504, 504, 630) yds of DK-weight cotton (100% cotton; 50 g; 126 yds) in beige [3]

420 yds (all sizes) of fingering-weight merino wool (100% merino wool; 100 g; 420 yds) in beige [1]

US Size 9 (5.5 mm) straight or circular needles, or size needed to obtain gauge

2 buttons, approx ¾" diameter

Stitch markers, stitch holders, tapestry needle

Gauge

14 sts and 21 rows = 4" in St st with 1 strand of each yarn held tog

Body

Note: Hold 1 strand of each yarn tog throughout.

CO 80 (84, 92, 96, 100) sts. Work in garter st (knit every row) for 14 (14, 16, 20, 20) rows. Change to St st, keeping first and last 5 sts in garter st throughout.

Work even until piece measures 8 (8½, 9½, 10, 12½)", ending with a WS row.

Next row (RS): K18 (19, 21, 22, 23), BO 6 sts for underarm, K32 (34, 38, 40, 42), BO 6 sts for underarm, K18 (19, 21, 22, 23).

Change to garter st.

Next row: Knit, casting on 16 (18, 22, 26, 28) sts over each underarm gap.

Next (buttonhole) row (RS): K2, YO, K2tog, knit to end.

Next row: Knit.

Next (dec) row: Knit, dec 18 (18, 20, 20, 22) sts evenly across—82 (90, 104, 116, 122) sts.

Work in garter st for 3 (3, 7, 9, 11) rows.

Next (dec) row: Knit, dec 14 (14, 16, 18, 20) sts evenly across—68 (76, 88, 98, 102) sts.

Work in garter st for 3 (3, 7, 9, 11) rows.

Next (dec) row: Knit, dec 12 (12, 14, 16, 18) sts evenly across—56 (64, 74, 82, 84) sts.

Work in garter st for 3 (3, 7, 9, 11) rows.

Next (dec) row: K2, YO, K2tog (buttonhole made), knit to end, dec 8 (10, 12, 14, 14) sts evenly across—48 (54, 62, 68, 70) sts.

Knit 2 rows. BO.

Finishing

Weave in ends. Block. Sew buttons opposite buttonholes.

• • • • • • • • • • •

Troublemaker Sweater

This sweater is influenced by the character Lotta (from Astrid Lindgren's book series). It's knit with a stitch that makes it really stretchy, so it will fit for quite some time. The girls' version is bit longer than the boys'.

SKILL LEVEL: Easy

Sizes

To fit ages 1 (2, 3–4, 5–6, 7–8, 10, 12) years

Chest: 23½ (26, 28¼, 30, 31½, 33, 34½)"

Length (girls): 15¾ (17¼, 19¾, 21¼, 22¾, 24½, 27½)"

Length (boys): 14 (15¾, 17¾, 19¼, 21, 22½, 24)"

Materials

Sport-weight alpaca (100% alpaca; 50 g; 209 yds) in the following amounts and colors:

Girls: 1254 (1463, 1672, 2090, 2299, 2508, 2717) yds in red-orange

Boys: 1045 (1254, 1463, 1672, 1881, 2299, 2508) yds in red-orange

US Size 8 (5 mm) 24" to 32" circular and double-pointed needles, or size needed to obtain gauge

US Size 4 (3.5 mm) 24" to 32" circular and double-pointed needles

Stitch markers, stitch holders, tapestry needle

Gauge

24 sts = 4" in rib patt using larger needle, unstretched

Body

Note: Yarn is held double throughout. Girls' and boys' versions are the same except for length.

With smaller needle, CO 144 (160, 176, 184, 192, 200, 208) sts. Pm and join, being careful not to twist the sts. Work in P1, K1 rib for 2" (start with a purl st).

Pm 72 (80, 88, 92, 96, 100, 104) sts from first marker to mark opposite side "seam." Change to larger needles.

Rnd 1: *K3, P1; rep from * around.

Rnd 2: P1, K1, *P3, K1; rep from * to last 2 sts, P2.

Work even in patt until piece measures 9¾ (11, 12¼, 13¾, 15, 16½, 19¼)" for girls and 7¾ (9½, 10½, 11¾, 13, 14½, 15¾)" for boys.

BO 3 sts after each marker—138 (154, 170, 178, 188, 194, 202) sts. Front and back should both beg and end with a purl st. Set aside.

Sleeves

With smaller dpns, CO 34 (38, 42, 42, 46, 46, 50) sts. Work in K1, P1 rib for 2".

Change to larger dpns.

Rnd 1: K1, P1, K1 (underside of sleeve), K1, *P1, K3; rep from * to last 2 sts, P1, K1.

Rnd 2: K1, P1, K1 (underside of sleeve), *P3, K1; rep from * to last 3 sts, P3.

Inc 1 st each side of 3 underside of sleeve sts every 1½ (2, 2½, 2¾, 3, 3½, 4)" a total of 3 times—40 (44, 48, 48, 52, 52, 56) sts, working new sts in patt.

Work even in patt until sleeve measures 7¾ (9¾, 11, 12½, 13¾, 15, 15¾)". Bind off 3 underside of sleeve sts—37 (41, 45, 45, 49, 49, 53) sts. Place rem sts on holder.

Yoke

Aligning underarms, knit next rnd across sleeve and body sts to join, pm at beg and end of each set of sleeve sts (4 markers total)—212 (236, 260, 268, 286, 292, 308) sts.

Next rnd: Work even in patt, knitting st before and after each marker.

Next (dec) rnd: *Work in patt to 3 sts before next marker; ssk, K2 (raglan sts), K2tog; rep from * for rem markers, work in patt to end—8 sts dec.

Rep last 2 rnds a total of 16 (17, 20, 20, 21, 22, 24) times—84 (100, 100, 108, 118, 116, 116) sts.

Change to smaller needles.

Next (dec) rnd: *Work in K1, P1 rib to 1 st before next marker, K2tog; rep from * around, work in K1, P1 rib to end—4 sts dec.

Work even in K1, P1 rib for 2". BO loosely.

A cute set knit in rib and fisherman's rib.

Sizes

To fit ages 0–6 months (6–12 months, 1–2 years, 3–4 years, 5–6 years, 7–8 years, 9–10 years)

TUNIC

Chest: 20½ (23, 29, 31, 33, 34½, 36)"

Length: 10¼ (14¼, 17, 18½, 20¾, 22½, 24)"

HAT

Circumference: 13¼ (13¼, 14½, 16, 17¼, 18½, 19½)"

LEG WARMERS

Length: 6¼ (6¼, 7, 7½, 8¼, 9¼, 10)"

Materials

DK-weight alpaca (100% alpaca; 50 g; 109 yds) in the following amounts and colors: [3]

A: 218 (327, 327, 436, 545, 654, 763) yds in purple

B and C: 109 (218, 218, 218, 327, 327, 327) yds each in green (B) and gold (C)

US Size 7 (4.5 mm) 16" circular and double-pointed needles, or size needed to obtain gauge

US Size 5 (3.75 mm) double-pointed needles, or size needed to obtain gauge

US Size E-4 (3.5 mm) crochet hook

2 buttons, approx ¾" diameter

Stitch markers, tapestry needle

Gauge

12 sts = 4" in fisherman's rib patt using larger needle

20 sts = 4" in St st using smaller needle

Bubble Tunic

Tunic is knit from the top down in 1 piece.

Body

With larger needle and B, CO 47 (53, 63, 67, 73, 77, 81) sts. Work in rows in K1, P1 rib for ¾ (¾, 1¼, 1¼, 1¼, 1½, 1½)", ending with a WS row.

Next row (RS): With C, *K1, YO; rep from * to last st, K1—93 (105, 125, 133, 145, 153, 161) sts.

Next row: *P1, K1; rep from * to last st, P1.

Work in rib patt until piece measures 2 (2¾, 3½, 4¼, 5¼, 6, 6¾)", ending with a WS row. Change to A. Beg fisherman's rib patt as follows:

Row 1 (RS): Sl 1, *K1, K1b; rep from * to last st, K1.

Row 2: Sl 1, *K1b, K1; rep from * to last st, K1.

Rep rows 1 and 2 once.

Next row: Work in patt for 16 (18, 22, 24, 26, 27, 28) sts, BO 16 (18, 20, 20, 22, 24, 26) sts, work in patt for 29 (33, 41, 45, 49, 51, 53) sts, BO 16 (18, 20, 20, 22, 24, 26) sts, work in patt for 16 (18, 22, 24, 26, 27, 28) sts—61 (69, 85, 93, 101, 105, 109) sts.

Work even in patt for 3 more rows. Pm and join, RS facing you, casting on 1 st at end of first rnd—62 (70, 86, 94, 102, 106, 110) sts. Cont in fisherman's rib patt in the rnd as follows:

Rnd 1: *K1, P1b; rep from * around.

Rnd 2: *K1b, P1; rep from * around.

Rep rnds 1 and 2 until piece measures 9½ (13½, 15¾, 17¼, 19¼, 21, 22½)", ending with rnd 2.

Work in K1, P1 rib for ¾ (¾, 1¼, 1¼, 1½, 1½, 1½)". BO loosely.

Finishing

With crochet hook, work in sc around back opening, working ch for each desired button loop. Fasten off. Weave in ends. Sew buttons opposite button loops.

Hat

With smaller dpns and C, CO 66 (66, 72, 80, 86, 92, 98) sts. Pm and join, being careful not to twist the sts. Work in K1, P1 rib for ¾ (¾, 1¼, 1¼, 1½, 1½, 1½)". Work in fisherman's rib patt in the rnd as follows:

Rnd 1: *K1, P1b; rep from * around.

Rnd 2: *K1b, P1; rep from * around.

Rep rnds 1 and 2 until piece measures 4¼ (5, 5½, 6¼, 6¾, 7, 7)", ending with rnd 1.

Work in K1, P1 rib for 1¼".

Next (dec) rnd: K1, *sl 2-K1-psso, K1, P1, K1; rep from * around, stopping at last st. Knit first and last st of rnd tog. Cut yarn, draw through rem sts, pull tight, and secure.

To finish, weave in ends. Block.

Leg Warmers

With smaller dpns and B, CO 26 (32, 36, 40, 44, 48, 52) sts. Pm and join, being careful not to twist the sts. Work in K1, P1 rib for 1¼ (1¼, 1½, 1½, 1½, 1½, 1½)". Work in fisherman's rib in the rnd as follows:

Rnd 1: *K1, P1b; rep from * around.

Rnd 2: *K1b, P1; rep from * around.

Rep rnds 1 and 2 until piece measures 5 (5, 5½, 6, 6¾, 7¾, 8½)", ending with rnd 1.

Work in K1, P1 rib for 1¼ (1¼, 1½, 1½, 1½, 1½, 1½)". BO loosely.

To finish, weave in ends. Block.

• • • • • • • • • •

Zigzag Sweater

The contrast between the zigzag pattern and the solid collar is part of this sweater's appeal. This pattern is made with slip stitches, and you only knit with one color per row, so this sweater is much easier than it might appear.

SKILL LEVEL: Intermediate

Gauge

25 sts and 32 rows = 4" in St st

24 sts and 50 rows = 4" in zigzag patt

32 sts and 36 rows = 4" in rib patt, unstretched

Body

With circular needle and A, CO 104 (112, 144, 152, 168, 176) sts. Pm and join, being careful not to twist the sts. Work in K1, P1 rib for ¾ (¾, 1¼, 1¼, 1½, 1½, 1½)"

Next rnd: Knit, pm 52 (56, 64, 72, 76, 84, 88) sts from first marker to mark opposite side "seam."

Work body chart (page 66) until piece measures 5 (6¾, 7½, 8¾, 9¾, 11¼, 12½)", ending with the second to last rnd of any color.

Next rnd: BO 5 sts for underarm, K15 (16, 19, 23, 23, 27, 27), BO 17 (19, 21, 21, 25, 25, 29) sts for front neck, K15 (16, 19, 23, 23, 27, 27), BO 5 sts for underarm, knit to end—77 (83, 97, 113, 117, 133, 137) sts. Set aside.

Sizes

To fit ages 0–3 months (6 months, 9–12 months, 2 years, 3–4 years, 5–6 years, 7–8 years)

Chest: 17½ (19, 20½, 24, 25, 27½, 29)"

Length: 9 (11, 13, 15, 16½, 18¾, 20½)"

Materials

Sport-weight merino wool (100% merino wool; 100 g; 415 yds) in the following amounts and colors: **2**

A: 415 (415, 415, 415, 830, 830, 830) yds in teal

B: 415 (415, 415, 415, 415, 415, 415) yds in green

C: 415 (415, 415, 415, 415, 415, 415) yds in cream

US Size 2½ (3 mm) 24" and 32" circular and double-pointed needles, or size needed to obtain gauge

Stitch markers, stitch holders, tapestry needle

Sleeves

With dpns and A, CO 32 (34, 36, 38, 40, 42, 44) sts. Pm and join, being careful not to twist the sts. Work in K1, P1 rib for ¾ (¾, 1¼, 1¼, 1½, 1½, 1½)". Change to St st.

Next rnd: Knit, inc 4 (6, 4, 6, 4, 6, 4) sts evenly around—36 (40, 40, 44, 44, 48, 48) sts. Work left sleeve chart (page 66) for approx 2 (2½, 1½, 2, 1¼, 1½, 1¼)", ending on the second to last rnd of any color.

Note: The number of rnds between increases is not necessarily the same as shown on chart for all sizes.

Next (inc) rnd: M1L, work in patt to end of rnd, M1R—2 sts inc.

Rep inc rnd, incorporating new sts into established patt and making sure to work inc rnd on the last rnd of a color each time every 2 (2½, 1½, 2, 1¼, 1½, 1¼)" a total of 2 (2, 4, 4, 6, 6, 8) times—40 (44, 48, 52, 56, 60, 64) sts.

Work even in patt until piece measures 5 (6¼, 7¾, 9, 10, 11½, 13)", ending with the second to last rnd of same color as body ended.

Next rnd: BO 3 sts, work in patt to last 2 sts, BO 2 sts—35 (39, 43, 47, 51, 55, 59) sts.

Rep to make right sleeve, following right sleeve chart (page 66).

Yoke

Aligning underarms and using same color as ended on body, knit next row across sleeve and body sts to join, pm at beg and end of each set of sleeve sts and CO 1 st on each side of each of the 4 markers at beg and end of sleeve sts (8 sts inc)—155 (169, 191, 215, 227, 251, 263) sts.

Note: The sts just CO (raglan sts) should be worked in rev St st throughout and slipped wyib on the first row of each color change.

Work chart 3 (page 66), beg with a WS row with a new color. On the last row of each color (every 4 rows), work dec row as follows:

Dec row (RS): *Work in patt to 3 sts before next marker; ssk, P2 (raglan sts), K2tog; rep from * for rem markers, work in patt to end—8 sts dec.

Make certain to keep work in patt as sts dec.

Rep dec row 13 (14, 17, 20, 21, 24, 25) times total—51 (57, 55, 55, 59, 59, 63) sts, ending with a RS row.

Change to A.

Next row (WS): P2tog, purl to 1 st before marker, K2 (raglan sts), purl across sleeve sts, dec 2 (3, 2, 2, 3, 3, 3) sts evenly across, K2 (raglan sts), purl across back, dec 8 (10, 10, 10, 10, 10, 12) sts evenly across, K2 (raglan sts), purl across sleeve sts, dec 2 (3, 2, 2, 3, 3, 3) sts evenly across, K2 (raglan sts), purl to last 2 sts, P2tog—37 (39, 39, 39, 41, 41, 43) sts. Do not BO.

Collar

With A, PU 7 sts every 1" along 1 side of neck opening, knit across rem 37 (39, 39, 39, 41, 41, 43) sts, PU 7 sts every 1" along opposite side of neck opening, making sure to end up with an odd number of sts. Work in K1, P1 rib, ending with K1, until collar is as wide as the lower opening. BO loosely.

Finishing

Overlap edges of collar and sew in place at lower edge of front neck. Sew gap under arms. Weave in ends. Block.

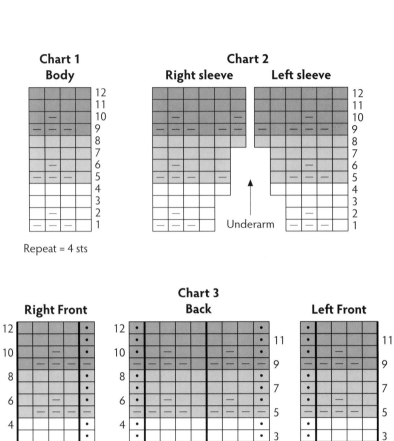

Skrollan's Kindergarten Set

A kindergarten set inspired by the '70s! The tunic has a simple construction and is knit top down. The colorful stripes will appeal to babies and kids alike.

SKILL LEVEL: Easy

Gauge

21 sts and 32 rows = 4" in St st using larger needle

Special Technique

Wrap and turn: Sl next st to RH needle, bring yarn to front/back (opposite side from previous st), sl st back to LH needle, return yarn to back/front.

Tunic

Piece is knit from top down in rows until stripes are complete, then in the rnd.

Yoke

With larger circular needle and A, CO 54 (54, 58, 58, 62) sts.

Rows 1–5: Knit.

Row 6: Purl, inc 16 (22, 24, 21, 23) sts evenly across.

Row 7 (RS): Change to C, purl.

Rows 8–12: Work in St st.

Row 13: Knit, inc 16 (22, 24, 21, 23) sts evenly across.

Row 14: Purl.

Row 15: Change to A, purl.

Rows 16–19: Work in St st.

Rep rows 6–19 a total of 3 (3, 3, 4, 4) times, alternating working rows

Sizes

To fit ages 3–6 months (6–12 months, 1–2 years, 3–4 years, 5–6 years)

TUNIC

Chest: 17 (23, 24½, 27, 28¼)"

Length: 13 (13¾, 15½, 18, 19½)"

TROUSERS

Waist: 17 (19, 20½, 23, 23½)"

Length: 13¾ (16, 18, 21½, 26¾)"

HAT

Circumference: 13¾ (15¼, 15¼, 16¾, 16¾)"

Materials

DK-weight merino wool (100% merino wool; 50 g; 153 yds) in the following amounts and colors: **3**

Girls:

A: 459 (612, 765, 918, 1071) yds in cream

B: 153 yds (all sizes) in pink

C: 306 (306, 459, 612, 765) yds in orange

Continued on page 68

Continued from page 67

Boys:

A: 459 (612, 765, 918, 1071) yds in blue

B: 306 (306, 459, 612, 765) yds in brown

C: 153 yds (all sizes) in yellow

US Size 5 (3.75 mm) 16", 24", and 32" circular and double-pointed needles, or size needed to obtain gauge

US Size 2½ (3 mm) 16" circular needle

4 (4, 4, 4, 5) buttons, ¾" diameter

Stitch markers, stitch holders, tapestry needle

7–14 with B or C each time through and ending last rep on row 14—150 (186, 202, 226, 246) sts.

Pm and join. Change to A.

Next rnd: Knit, CO 6 sts between first and last st of rnd, pm in center of these new sts for center back—156 (192, 208, 232, 252) sts.

Knit 7 (11, 17, 7, 11) rnds.

Body

Next row (RS): With A, K23 (30, 32, 35, 38), place next 32 (36, 40, 46, 50) sts on holder for sleeve, CO 2 sts at underarm, K46 (60, 64, 70, 76), place next 32 (36, 40, 46, 50) sts on holder for second sleeve, CO 2 sts at underarm, knit to end—96 (124, 132, 144, 156) sts for body. Pm in center of 2 CO sts at each underarm to mark side "seams." Pm and join into rnd.

Work in St st for 1¼ (1½, 1½, 2, 2¼)".

Next (inc) rnd: *Knit to 1 st before side marker, M1L, K2, M1R; rep from * on opposite side, knit to end—4 sts inc.

Rep inc rnd every 1¼ (1½, 1½, 2, 2¼)" a total of 3 (4, 5, 5, 6) times—108 (140, 152, 164, 180) sts. Work in garter st (knit 1 rnd, purl 1 rnd) for 1½". BO.

Sleeves

Place 32 (36, 40, 46, 50) held sleeve sts on dpns, join A and CO 2 sts at underarm—34 (38, 42, 48, 52) sts. Pm and join. Work in St st until piece measures 3 (4, 5, 7, 9)". Work in garter st for 1½". BO.

Finishing

Sew gap under arms.

Front Bands

With A, PU 30 (32, 34, 38, 42) sts along left side of center front for button band (or side desired). Work in garter st (knit every row) for 1". BO.

On opposite side, PU same number of sts and work in garter st for ½".

Next (buttonhole) row: K6 (4, 6, 6, 7), *YO, K2tog, K4 (5, 5, 6, 5); rep from * to end.

Work even in garter st until band measures 1". BO.

Lap buttonhole band over button band and sew lower edges tog.

Weave in ends. Block. Sew buttons opposite buttonholes.

Hat

With larger circular needle and A, CO 72 (80, 80, 88, 88) sts. Pm and join, being careful not to twist the sts.

Rnds 1–5: Knit.

Rnd 6: Change to B, purl.

Rep rnds 1–6 a total of 5 (5, 6, 7, 8) times, alternating between B and C on each rep of rnd 6.

Shape Crown

Note: Change to dpns when needed.

Rnds 1–4: Knit.

Rnd 5: *K6, K2tog; rep from * around—63 (70, 70, 77, 77) sts.

Rnd 6: Change to B (or C), purl.

Rnds 7–10: Knit.

Rnd 11: *K5, K2tog; rep from * around—54 (60, 60, 66, 66) sts.

Rnd 12: Change to C (or B), purl.

Rep rnds 1–12, working 1 less st before the dec on rnds 5 and 11 each time as established until 18 (20, 20, 22, 22) sts rem.

Next rnd: *K2tog; rep from * around—9 (10, 10, 11, 11) sts.

Knit 5 rnds.

Finishing

Cut yarn, draw through rem sts, pull tight, and secure.

Trousers

With smaller circular needle and C for girls or B for boys, CO 88 (96, 104, 112, 120) sts. Pm and join, being careful not to twist the sts. Place 2 additional markers, each 44 (48, 52, 56, 60) sts apart, to mark center front and back. Work in K2, P2 rib for ½".

Next (eyelet) rnd: *K2, YO, P2tog; rep from * around.

Work in K2, P2 rib for 1½ (1½, 2, 2, 2)". Change to larger circular needle and St st. Work even until piece measures 5½ (7, 7½, 7¾, 8¼)".

Short Rows for Back

Row 1: Work in St st to 6 (7, 8, 9, 9) sts past center-back marker, wrap and turn.

Row 2: Work in St st to 6 (7, 8, 9, 9) sts on opposite side of center-back marker, wrap and turn.

Row 3: Work in St st to 12 (14, 16, 18, 18) sts past center-back marker, wrap and turn.

Row 4: Work in St st to 12 (14, 16, 18, 18) sts on opposite side of center-back marker, wrap and turn.

Row 5: Work in St st to 18 (21, 24, 27, 27) sts past center-back marker, wrap and turn.

Row 6: Work in St st to 18 (21, 24, 27, 27) sts on opposite side of center-back marker, wrap and turn.

Work in the Round

Shape crotch as follows:

Next (inc) rnd: *Knit to 2 sts before center-front marker, M1, K4, M1; rep from * on back—4 sts inc.

Next rnd: Knit.

Rep last 2 rnds a total of 3 times—100 (108, 116, 124, 132) sts.

BO 4 sts at center front and 4 sts at center back—92 (100, 108, 116, 124) sts.

Legs

Place half of rem sts on dpns for first leg—46 (50, 54, 58, 62) sts. Pm and join. Place rem sts on holder for second leg. Work even in St st until piece measures 6¼ (7, 8½, 11¾, 16½)" from BO.

Next rnd: Knit, dec 12 sts evenly around—34 (38, 42, 46, 50) sts.

Work in garter st (knit 1 rnd, purl 1 rnd) for 1". BO. Rep for other leg.

Finishing

Sew crotch seam closed.

Drawstring

With smaller dpns and A, CO 4 sts. Work in I-cord (page 109) as follows to approx 20" longer than waist measurement:

Knit across row, do not turn, slide sts to opposite end of dpn, pull gently to tighten.

Rep for patt.

Thread through eyelet rnd.

Weave in ends. Block.

Ahoy Vest

You'll love the construction of this sailor-inspired vest! It's knit seamlessly to the underarms, and then the yoke is knit flat with the sleeve caps incorporated directly into the front and back instead of being knit separately and sewn in place.

SKILL LEVEL: Easy

Sizes

To fit ages 3 months (6 months, 1 year, 2 years, 3–4 years, 5–6 years, 7–8 years)

Chest: 19 (19½, 21, 22½, 25, 28, 30½)"

Length: 9 (11, 12½, 13¾, 15, 16, 17¼)"

Materials

DK-weight cotton blend (70% cotton, 30% merino wool; 50 g; 129 yds) in the following amounts and colors: 🧶

A: 258 (258, 387, 387, 516, 516, 645) yds in brown

B: 129 yds (all sizes) in white

US Size 6 (4 mm) 16" to 24" circular needle, or size needed to obtain gauge

US Size E-4 (3.5 mm) crochet hook

2 buttons, approx ¾" diameter

Stitch markers, stitch holders, tapestry needle

Gauge

19 sts and 28 rows = 4" in St st

Body

With A, CO 92 (96, 104, 112, 124, 136, 148) sts. Pm and join, being careful not to twist the sts. Pm 46 (48, 52, 56, 62, 68, 74) sts from first marker to mark opposite side "seam."

Purl 1 rnd.

Knit 2 rnds.

Change to B. Knit 1 rnd, purl 1 rnd.

Change to A. Knit 2 rnds.

Change to B. Knit 1 rnd, purl 1 rnd.

Change to A. Work even in St st until piece measures 5½ (7, 8, 8¾, 9½, 10¼, 11)". Bind off 4 sts each side of each marker (8 sts total per side) for underarms—76 (80, 88, 96, 108, 120, 132) sts.

Back

With A, CO 18 (20, 22, 24, 26, 28, 30) sts for sleeve, pm, knit across 38 (40, 44, 48, 54, 60, 66) back sts, pm, CO 18 (20, 22, 24, 26, 28, 30) sts for second sleeve—74 (80, 88, 96, 106, 116, 126) sts.

Next row: Knit.

Shape Neck and Shoulders

Row 1 (dec row, RS): With A, *knit to 2 sts before marker, ssk, K2tog; rep from * across, knit to end—4 sts dec.

Row 2: With A, purl.

Rows 3 and 4: Rep rows 1 and 2.

Row 5: With B, knit.

Row 6: With B, knit.

Rep rows 1–6 a total of 3 times. Rep rows 1 and 2 only until dec row has been worked a total of 11 (12, 13, 15, 16, 18, 20) times—30 (32, 36, 36, 42, 44, 46) sts.

Knit 1 row. BO.

Front

Work as for back.

Finishing

Sew shoulders seams, leaving approx 1" open at inside edge on each side for buttons.

With crochet hook and A, work ch for button loops on each side of neck. Sew buttons opposite button loops. Weave in ends. Block.

Sailor Sweater

Choose a wool-cotton blend for this easy, summery sweater to make it cozy and warm all year long.

SKILL LEVEL: Easy

Sizes

To fit ages 1 (2, 3–4, 5–6, 7–8, 10, 12) years

Chest: 20½ (23, 25, 27½, 30, 31½, 33)"

Length: 11¾ (15¾, 17, 17¾, 19, 20½, 22)"

Materials

DK-weight cotton blend (70% cotton, 30% merino wool; 50 g; 129 yds) in the following amounts and colors 🔵**3**

A: 258 (387, 516, 645, 774, 903, 1032) yds in white

B: 129 yds (all sizes) in blue

C: 129 yds (all sizes) in orange

US Size 6 (4 mm) 24" to 32" circular and double-pointed needles, or size needed to obtain gauge

US Size 3 (3.25 mm) 24" to 32" circular and double-pointed needles

Stitch markers, stitch holders, tapestry needle

Gauge

19 sts and 28 rows = 4" in St st using larger needle

Body

With smaller circular needle and A, CO 98 (110, 122, 130, 142, 150, 162) sts. Pm and join, being careful not to twist the sts. Pm 49 (55, 61, 65, 71, 75, 81) sts from first marker to mark opposite side "seam."

Work in K1, P1 rib for 1½ (1½, 1½, 2, 2, 2, 2)". Change to larger circular needle.

Knit 4 rnds. Beg color patt as follows:

Note: Use a double strand of color B or C, alternating colors every rep of patt. Front and back both beg and end with sl 1. This keeps patt balanced when front and back are divided.

Rnd 1: With B (or C), *sl 1 wyib, K1; rep from * around to 1 st before side marker, sl 1 wyib; rep from * around.

Rnd 2: With same color as last rnd, *sl 1 wyif, P1; rep from * around to 1 st before side marker, sl 1 wyif; rep from * around.

Rnds 3–12: With A, knit.

Rep rnds 1–12 until the piece measures 8 (11¼, 12, 12½, 13¼, 14½, 15¼)".

Front

Cont in patt as follows over 49 (55, 61, 65, 71, 75, 81) front sts only. Leave rem sts for back on holder.

Row 1 (RS): With B (or C), *sl 1 wyib, K1; rep from * to last st, sl 1 wyib.

Row 2: Rep row 1.

Rows 3–12: With A, work in St st.

Rep rows 1–12 until piece measures 9½ (13¼, 14½, 14¾, 16, 17¼, 18½)".

Change to smaller circular needle. Work in K1, P1 rib, ending with K1, until piece measures 11¾ (15¾, 17, 17¾, 19, 20½, 22)". BO.

Back

Work as for front.

Assembly

Sew 10 (13, 15, 16, 18, 20, 22) shoulder sts on each side to join front and back, leaving rem center sts open for neck.

Sleeves

With larger dpns and A, PU 38 (44, 50, 52, 56, 60, 68) sts around armhole, pm and join. To match stripes, count rnds of St st from the last stripe before front and back were separated down to the stripe below. Knit same number of rnds in A, then cont as follows:

Rnd 1: *Sl 1 wyib, K1; rep from * around.

Rnd 2: *Sl 1 wyif, P1; rep from * around.

Rnds 3–12: With A, knit.

Rep rnds 1–12 and AT THE SAME TIME, work dec rnd every 3½ (2, 2¼, 2, 2, 1¾, 1)" a total of 2 (4, 4, 5, 6, 8, 11) times—34 (36, 42, 42, 44, 44, 46) sts.

Dec rnd: K1, K2tog, knit to last 3 sts, ssk, K1—2 sts dec.

Work even until piece measures 7 (8½, 9¾, 11½, 12½, 14, 15)". Change to smaller needles. Work in K1, P1 rib for 1½ (1½, 1½, 2, 2, 2, 2)". BO.

Finishing

Weave in ends. Block.

• • • • • • • • • • •

Sizes

To fit ages 6 months (1 year, 2–3 years, 4–5 years, 6–8 years)

COAT

Chest: 19 (21, 25, 26½, 28¼)"

Length: 14 (15¾, 17, 19¼, 21¼)", excluding collar

HAT

Circumference: Approx 13 (13¾, 14½, 15½, 16)"

Materials

415 (830, 830, 830, 1245) yds of sport-weight merino wool (100% merino wool; 100 g; 415 yds) in color raspberry [2]

545 (654, 763, 872, 981) yds of DK-weight alpaca (100% alpaca; 50 g; 109 yds) in raspberry [3]

US Size 10 (6 mm) 32" to 40" circular needle, or size needed to obtain gauge

US Size 8 (5 mm) 16" and 32" circular and double-pointed needles, or size needed to obtain gauge

US Size 6 (4 mm) 16" circular needle

7 buttons, approx ¾" diameter

Stitch markers, stitch holders, tapestry needle

Lil' Miss Coat and Hat

Dressed up or down, a set like this is a must for every little miss! The combination of a tweed's hold and an alpaca's softness is perfect for these garments. Be sure to follow the instructions closely since the coat is worked side to side from cuff to cuff.

SKILL LEVEL: Experienced

Gauge

16 sts and 22 rows = 4" in St st using size 8 needle with 1 strand of each yarn held tog

13 sts and 26 rows = 4" in garter st using size 10 needle with 1 strand of each yarn held tog

Coat

Note: Coat is knit from cuff to cuff. Hold 1 strand of each yarn tog throughout.

Coat begins at right sleeve.

Right sleeve

With size 8 needle, CO 28 (30, 34, 36, 38) sts. Knit 2 rows. Change to size 10 needle. Work even in garter st (knit every row) until piece measures 4¾ (6, 7½, 9, 10½)".

Body

CO 30 (34, 36, 42, 48) sts at beg of next 2 rows, pm between sleeve sts and sts just CO on each side—88 (98, 106, 120, 134) sts. Knit 5 rows.

Short rows 1 and 2: Knit to first marker, wrap and turn, knit back.

Row 3 (RS): K5, M1, knit to end—1 st inc.

Short rows 4 and 5: Rep short rows 1 and 2 to shape other side.

Row 6 (WS): Rep row 3.

Rep rows 1–6 a total of 3 times—94 (104, 112, 126, 140) sts.

Knit 3 (5, 5, 5, 5) rows. Cont as follows:

Short rows 1 and 2: Knit to first marker, wrap and turn, knit back.

Row 3 (WS): Knit to end.

Short rows 4 and 5: Rep short rows 1 and 2 to shape other side.

Row 6 (RS): Rep row 3.

Rep rows 1–6 a total of 1 (1, 2, 2, 2) times—94 (104, 112, 126, 140) sts.

Next row (WS): K47 (52, 56, 63, 70) sts for back. Place on holder. CO 6 (7, 7, 8, 9) sts for collar, knit to end of row for right front—53 (59, 63, 71, 79) sts.

Right Front

Knit 2 (4, 4, 4, 4) rows.

Short rows 1 and 2: Knit to marker, wrap and turn, knit back.

Rep last 2 rows a total of 1 (1, 1, 1, 2) times.

Size 4–5 years only:

Knit 4 rows.

Buttonhole Band

Knit 6 rows. Mark location of 7 evenly spaced buttonholes. Do not place a buttonhole on collar sts.

Next (buttonhole) row: Knit, working K2tog, YO at each marker.

Work in garter st for 5 rows more. BO.

Left Front

With size 10 needle, CO 53 (59, 63, 71, 79) sts. Work in garter st for 12 rows. Pm 30 (34, 36, 42, 48) sts from lower edge.

Size 4–5 years only:

Knit 4 rows.

All Sizes:

Short rows 1 and 2: Knit to marker, wrap and turn, knit back.

Rep last 2 rows a total of 1 (1, 1, 1, 2) times.

Knit 3 (5, 5, 5, 5) rows. BO 6 (7, 7, 8, 9) collar sts—47 (52, 56, 63, 70) sts. Set aside.

Back

CO 6 (7, 7, 8, 9) sts for collar at beg of held back sts, with RS facing you. Knit to end of row across rem K47 (52, 56, 63, 70) back sts—53 (59, 63, 71, 79) sts.

Short rows 1 and 2: *Knit to marker, wrap and turn, knit back.

Rep last 2 rows a total of 1 (1, 1, 1, 2) time.**

Work in garter st for 12 rows.

Rep from * to **. BO 6 (7, 7, 8, 9) collar sts—47 (52, 56, 63, 70) sts.

Join Back and Left Front

Next row (RS): Join yarn and knit across all rem sts on left front and back—94 (104, 112, 126, 140) sts.

Short rows 1 and 2: Knit to first marker, wrap and turn, knit back.

Row 3 (WS): Knit to end.

Short rows 4 and 5: Rep short rows 1 and 2 to shape other side.

Row 6 (RS): Rep row 3.

Rep rows 1–6 a total of 1 (1, 2, 2, 2) times—94 (104, 112, 126, 140) sts.

Knit 3 (5, 5, 5, 5) rows. Cont as follows:

Short rows 1 and 2: Knit to first marker, wrap and turn, knit back.

Row 3 (RS): K5, K2tog, knit to end—1 st dec.

Short rows 4 and 5: Rep short rows 1 and 2 to shape other side.

Row 6 (WS): Rep row 3.

Rep rows 1–6 a total of 3 times—88 (98, 106, 120, 134) sts.

Knit 5 rows.

BO 30 (34, 36, 42, 48) sts at beg of next 2 rows—28 (30, 34, 36, 38) sts.

Sleeve

Work as for first sleeve, changing to size 8 needle for last 2 rows. BO.

Finishing

Sew side and sleeve seams. Weave in ends. Block. Sew buttons opposite buttonholes.

Hat

Note: Hold 1 strand of each yarn tog throughout.

With size 6 needle, CO 62 (66, 72, 76, 80) sts. Pm and join, being careful not to twist sts. Work in K1, P1 rib for 1½". Change to size 8 needle.

Next rnd: Knit, inc 10 (14, 16, 20, 24) sts evenly around—72 (80, 88, 96, 104) sts.

Pm every 9 (10, 11, 12, 13) sts—8 markers total.

Work even in St st until piece measures 2½ (2¾, 3, 3½, 4)".

Shape Crown

Note: Change to dpns when needed.

Rnd 1: *Knit to 2 sts before marker, ssk, sl marker, K2tog; rep from * around—16 sts dec.

Rnds 2–4: Knit.

Rep rnds 1–4 a total of 3 (4, 4, 5, 5) times—24 (16, 24, 16, 24) sts.

Knit 3 rnds.

Sizes 1 and 4–5 years only:

Next rnd: *K2tog; rep from * around—8 sts.

Cut yarn, draw through rem sts, pull tight, and secure.

All other sizes only:

Next rnd: *Sl 2 kw, K2, psso; rep from * around—12 sts.

Cut yarn, draw through rem sts, pull tight, and secure.

Finishing

Weave in ends. Block.

· · · · · · · · · · ·

Sizes

To fit ages 3 months (6 months, 1 year, 2 years)

JUMPSUIT

Chest: 17½ (20, 22, 23½)"

Length: 16 (18, 20, 22½)", excluding collar

HAT

Circumference: 12 (13¾, 15¼, 16¾)"

Materials

DK-weight cotton blend (70% cotton, 30% wool; 50 g; 129 yds) in the following amounts and colors: (3)

A: 258 (387, 516, 645) yds in gray

B: 129 (258, 258, 258) yds in orange

US Size 4 (3.5 mm) 16" and 32" circular and double-pointed needles, or size needed to obtain gauge

5 (5, 6, 6) buttons

Stitch markers, stitch holders, tapestry needle

Melker's Summer Jumpsuit and Hat

This easy-knit set is really great during summer. It keeps your child warm, yet it is airy and nice with short sleeves and short legs. The hat adds a colorful touch.

SKILL LEVEL: Easy

Gauge

21 sts and 31 rows = 4" in St st

Special Technique

Wrap and turn: Sl next st to RH needle, bring yarn to front/back (opposite side from previous st), sl st back to LH needle, return yarn to back/front.

Jumpsuit

Jumpsuit is worked top down in 1 piece.

Collar

With B, CO 54 (54, 58, 58) sts. Work in garter st (knit every row) for 1", ending with a RS row.

Yoke

Change to A.

Row 1 (WS): Purl, inc 16 (20, 22, 24) sts evenly across—70 (74, 80, 82) sts.

Row 2: Purl.

Rows 3–7: Work in St st.

Row 8 (RS): Knit, inc 16 (20, 22, 24) sts evenly across—86 (94, 102, 106) sts.

Row 9: Knit.

Rows 10–14: Work in St st.

Work rows 1–14 a total of 3 times, ending with row 10 on last rep—150 (174, 190, 202) sts.

Work in St st for 3 (5, 9, 13) rows.

Next row (RS): K20 (23, 26, 28) for front, place next 32 (38, 40, 42) sts on holder for sleeve, CO 2 sts at underarm, K46 (52, 58, 62) for back, place next 32 (38, 40, 42) sts on holder for sleeve, CO 2 sts at underarm, K20 (23, 26, 28) for front—90 (102, 114, 122) body sts.

Body

Work in St st until piece measures 11 (12½, 13¾, 15½)". CO 6 sts for center front and join, pm in center of these 6 sts—96 (108, 120, 128) sts. Pm 48 (54, 60, 64) sts from first marker to mark center back.

Work even in St st until piece measures 11¾ (13¼, 14½, 16¼)".

Short Rows for Back

Row 1: Work in St st to 5 (6, 7, 7) sts past center-back marker, wrap and turn.

Row 2: Work in St st to 5 (6, 7, 7) sts on opposite side of center-back marker, wrap and turn.

Row 3: Work in St st to 10 (12, 14, 14) sts past center-back marker, wrap and turn.

Row 4: Work in St st to 10 (12, 14, 14) sts on opposite side of center-back marker, wrap and turn.

Row 5: Work in St st to 15 (18, 21, 21) sts past center-back marker, wrap and turn.

Row 6: Work in St st to 15 (18, 21, 21) sts on opposite side of center-back marker, wrap and turn.

Row 7: Work in St st to 20 (24, 28, 28) sts past center-back marker, wrap and turn.

Row 8: Work in St st to 20 (24, 28, 28) sts on opposite side of center-back marker, wrap and turn.

Work in the Round

Shape crotch as follows:

Next (inc) rnd: *K3, M1R, knit to 3 sts before next marker, M1L, K3; rep from * around—4 sts inc.

Next rnd: Knit.

Rep last 2 rnds a total of 3 times—108 (120, 132, 140) sts.

BO 6 sts at center front and 6 sts at center back—96 (108, 120, 128) sts.

Legs

Place half of rem sts on dpns for first leg—48 (54, 60, 64) sts. Pm and join. Place rem sts on holder for second leg. Work even in St st until piece measures 2¼ (3, 4, 4¾)" from BO.

Next (dec) rnd: Knit, dec 8 (10, 10, 10) sts evenly around—40 (44, 50, 54) sts.

Change to B. Work in garter st (knit 1 rnd, purl 1 rnd) for 1". BO. Rep for other leg.

Sleeves

Place held 32 (38, 40, 42) sts on dpns. CO 2 sts at underarm, pm in center of these 2 sts and join—34 (40, 42, 44) sts.

Work in St st until piece measures 2 (2¾, 3¾, 4)".

Next (dec) rnd: Knit, dec 4 (4, 6, 6) sts evenly around—30 (36, 36, 38) sts. Change to B. Work in garter st for 1". BO.

Finishing

Sew crotch seam closed. Sew gap under arms.

Front Bands

With A, PU 21 sts every 4" along left side of center front for button band (or side desired). Work in garter st for 1". BO.

On opposite side, PU same number of sts and work in garter st for ½". Mark location of 5 (5, 6, 6) buttonholes, evenly spaced.

Next row: *Knit to marker, K2tog, YO; rep from * across, knit to end.

Work even in garter st until band measures 1". BO.

Lap buttonhole band over button band and sew lower edges tog. Weave in ends. Block. Sew buttons opposite buttonholes.

Hat

With B, CO 64 (72, 80, 88) sts. Pm and join, being careful not to twist the sts. Work in St st until piece measures 4¼ (4¾, 5, 5½)". Change to A.

Shape Crown

Note: Change to dpns when needed.

Rnd 1: *K6, K2tog; rep from * around—56 (63, 70, 77) sts.

Rnd 2 and all even rnds through 10: Knit.

Rnd 3: *K5, K2tog; rep from * around—48 (54, 60, 66) sts.

Rnd 5: *K4, K2tog; rep from * around—40 (45, 50, 55) sts.

Rnd 7: *K3, K2tog; rep from * around—32 (36, 40, 44) sts.

Rnd 9: *K2, K2tog; rep from * around—24 (27, 30, 33) sts.

Rnd 11: *K1, K2tog; rep from * around—16 (18, 20, 22) sts.

Rnd 12: *K2tog; rep from * around—8 (9, 10, 11) sts.

Rep rnd 12 until 4 sts rem, adjusting number of decs as needed. Work in I-cord (page 109) as follows on rem sts until long enough to form a small loop:

Knit across row, do not turn, slide sts to opposite end of dpn, pull gently to tighten.

Rep for patt.

BO and sew end in place in a loop.

Ties (optional)

With A, PU 4 sts at lower side of hat, approx ½" up from edge. Work in I-cord as above until cord is desired length. Rep on opposite side.

Finishing

Weave in ends. Block.

Small and Clever Set

This set, which is cute as well as functional, is all about construction. You knit the hat from cord to cord, the mittens from tip to tip, and the booties sideways!

SKILL LEVEL: Easy

Sizes

To fit ages 0–3 (6–12) months

HAT

Circumference: Approx 12–13 (14–16)" (stretches to fit)

MITTENS

Circumference: 5 (7)"

BOOTIES

Circumference: Approx 3 (4)" (stretches to fit)

Materials

Worsted-weight merino wool (100% merino wool; 100 g; 220 yds) in the following amounts and colors: [4]

A: 220 yds in gray *or* yellow

B: 220 yds in red *or* gray

US Size 6 (4 mm) 24" circular and double-pointed needles, or size needed to obtain gauge

Stitch markers, tapestry needle

Gauge

18 sts = 4" in St st

Special Technique

Wrap and turn: Sl next st to RH needle, bring yarn to front/back (opposite side from previous st), sl st back to LH needle, return yarn to back/front.

Hat

The hat is knit sideways from cord to cord. With dpns and A, CO 3 sts. Knit in I-cord (page 109) as follows for 6 (6¼)":

Row 1: Knit across row, do not turn, slide sts to opposite end of dpn, pull gently to tighten.

Rep row 1 for patt.

Purl next row.

Next row (RS): K1, M1, K1, M1, K1—5 sts. Pm on either side of center 3 sts.

Next row: K1, P3, K1.

Shape as follows, keeping center 3 sts in St st:

Row 1 (RS): Sl 1, knit to marker, M1R, K3, M1L, knit to end—2 sts inc.

Row 2: Sl 1, knit to marker, P3, knit to end.

Rep rows 1 and 2 until there are 39 (43) sts, ending with row 2.

Change to B. Remove markers. Knit 2 rows.

Size 6–12 months only:

Short rows 1 and 2: K38, wrap and turn, knit to end.

All Sizes:

Short rows 1 and 2 (3 and 4): K33, wrap and turn, knit to end.

Short rows 3 and 4 (5 and 6): K28, wrap and turn, knit to end.

Short rows 5 and 6 (7 and 8): K23, wrap and turn, knit to end.

Short rows 7 and 8 (9 and 10): K19, wrap and turn, knit to end.

Rows 9 and 10 (11 and 12): Knit.

Short rows 11 and 12 (13 and 14): K19, wrap and turn, knit to end.

Short rows 13 and 14 (15 and 16): K23, wrap and turn, knit to end.

Short rows 15 and 16 (17 and 18): K28, wrap and turn, knit to end.

Short rows 17 and 18 (19 and 20): K33, wrap and turn, knit to end.

Size 6-12 months only:

Short rows 1 and 2: K38, wrap and turn, knit to end.

All Sizes

Knit 2 rows.

Change to A. Pm each side of center 3 sts once more. Shape as follows:

Row 1 (RS): Knit to 2 sts before marker, ssk, K3, K2tog, knit to end—2 sts dec.

Row 2: Sl 1, knit to marker, P3, knit to end.

Rep rows 1 and 2 until there are 5 sts, ending with row 2.

Next row: Ssk, K1, K2tog—3 sts.

Next row: Purl.

Work in I-cord as follows for 6 (6¼)":

Knit across row, do not turn, slide sts to opposite end of dpn, pull gently to tighten.

Rep for patt.

BO. Weave in ends. Block.

Booties

With A, CO 24 (28) sts.

Knit 8 (12) rows.

Short rows 1 and 2: K14 (16), wrap and turn, knit to end.

Short rows 3 and 4: K13 (15), wrap and turn, knit to end.

Cont as set, working 1 less st before wrap and turn each time, for a total of 11 (12) short rows. BO first 3 (4) sts—21 (24) sts.

Change to B. Knit 13 (15) rows.

With A, CO 3 (4) sts and knit across—24 (28) sts. Cont as follows:

Short rows 1 and 2: K1, wrap and turn, knit to end.

Short rows 3 and 4: K2, wrap and turn, knit to end.

Cont as set, working 1 more st before wrap and turn each time, for a total of 11 (12) short rows. Knit 8 (12) rows. BO.

Sew seam along bottom of foot. Weave in ends. Block.

Mittens

Mittens are knit from tip to tip, with I-cord in between.

First Mitten

With dpns and A, CO 8 sts. Pm and join, being careful not to twist the sts. Change to B after 1".

Rnd 1: Knit.

Rnd 2: K1, M1L, knit to last st on needle 2, M1R, K2, M1L, knit to last st, M1R, K1—4 sts inc.

Rep last 2 rnds a total of 4 (6) times—24 (32) sts.

Work even in St st until piece measures 3 (3½)".

Next (dec) rnd: Knit, dec 6 sts evenly around—18 (26) sts.

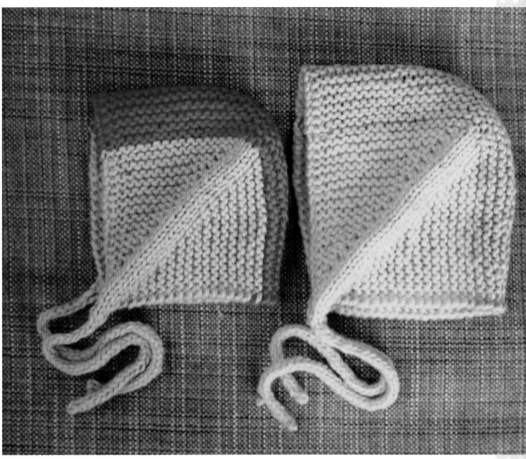

Work in K1, P1 rib for 1¼ (1½)".

Next rnd: K1, BO to last 2 sts—3 sts rem.

Work in I-cord (page 109) as follows until cord measures 21½ (25½)":

Knit across row, do not turn, slide sts to opposite end of dpn, pull gently to tighten.

Rep for patt.

Do not BO.

Second Mitten

CO 15 (23) sts—18 (26) sts.

Work in K1, P1 rib for 1¼ (1½)".

Work in St st, inc 6 sts evenly on first rnd—24 (32) sts.

Work even in St st until piece measures 2½ (2¾)" from beg of rib.

Next rnd: K1, K2tog, knit to last 3 sts on needle 2, ssk, K2, K2tog, knit to last 3 sts, ssk, K1—4 sts dec.

Next rnd: Knit.

Rep last 2 rnds until 8 sts rem. Cut yarn, draw through rem sts, pull tight, and secure.

Finishing

Weave in ends. Block.

· · · · · · · · · ·

Sizes

To fit ages 0–3 months (6–12 months, 1 year, 2 years)

Chest: 18 (21, 24½, 26)"

Length: 21¼ (25, 28¼, 31½)", excluding collar

Materials

DK-weight merino wool (100% merino wool; 50 g; 153 yds) in the following amounts and colors:

A: 765 (1224, 1530, 1836) yds in gray

B: 153 (153, 153, 153) yds in navy

C: 153 (153, 153, 153) yds in light blue

D: 153 (153, 153, 153) yds in orange

E: 153 (153, 153, 153) yds in gold

US Size 9 (5.5 mm) 16" and 32" circular and double-pointed needles, or size needed to obtain gauge

6 buttons, approx ¾" diameter

Stitch markers, stitch holders, tapestry needle

Zzz Jumpsuit

The Zzz Jumpsuit, as the name suggests, is made for sleeping. It has practical pockets that fold up and over to create built-in socks and mittens.

SKILL LEVEL: Easy

Gauge

15 sts and 32 rows = 4" in garter st with yarn held double

Special Technique

Wrap and turn: Sl next st to RH needle, bring yarn to front/back (opposite side from previous st), sl st back to LH needle, return yarn to back/front.

Yoke

Note: Yarn is held double throughout. On yoke, hold 1 strand of A and alternate a strand of B, C, D, or E approx every 2 to 6 rows. For rest of jumpsuit, hold 2 strands of A.

CO 40 (44, 48, 50) sts. Knit 12 (12, 14, 14) rows. AT THE SAME TIME, make buttonhole after first 4 rows, then every 14 (16, 18, 20) rows throughout as follows: K3, YO, K2tog, knit to end.

Next (inc) row (RS): Knit, inc 20 (26, 30, 34) sts evenly across, making sure not to work inc over first or last 6 sts (front bands)—60 (70, 78, 84) sts.

Knit 7 (9, 9, 11) rows.

Next (inc) row (RS): Knit, inc 16 (18, 24, 26) sts evenly across—76 (88, 102, 110) sts.

Knit 9 (11, 11, 13) rows.

Next (inc) row (RS): Knit, inc 20 (24, 26, 28) sts evenly across—96 (112, 128, 138) sts.

Knit 7 (9, 9, 11) rows.

Next (inc) row (RS): Knit, inc 22 (26, 28, 30) sts evenly across—118 (138, 156, 168) sts. Change to 2 strands of A and St st, cont to work buttonholes as established and work first and last 6 sts in garter st (knit every row).

Work even in patt for ½ (½, ½, ¾)", ending with a WS row.

Body

Next row (RS): K20 (23, 26, 28) for front, place next 22 (26, 29, 31) sts on holder for sleeve, CO 6 sts at underarm, K34 (40, 46, 50) for back, place next 22 (26, 29, 31) sts on holder for sleeve, CO 6 sts at underarm, K20 (23, 26, 28) for front—86 (98, 110, 118) body sts.

Work even in St st until piece measures 11½ (13¼, 14, 15¼)" from first inc row, ending with a WS row.

Join lower edge of front bands as follows:

Next row (RS): Knit to last 6 sts, place on spare needle and hold these 6 sts behind work. Pm and join.

On next rnd, purl each of these band sts tog with corresponding st held in back from other band, knit rem sts—80 (92, 104, 112) sts.

Knit 3 rnds, keeping 6 band sts in garter st (knit 1 rnd, purl 1 rnd). Change to St st. Pm in center of 6 band sts and pm 40 (46, 52, 56) sts from first marker to mark center back. Rnds beg at center front.

Short Rows for Back

Row 1: Work in St st to 6 sts past center-back marker, wrap and turn.

Row 2: Work in St st to 6 sts on opposite side of center-back marker, wrap and turn.

Row 3: Work in St st to 12 sts past center-back marker, wrap and turn.

Row 4: Work in St st to 12 sts on opposite side of center-back marker, wrap and turn.

Row 5: Work in St st to 18 sts past center-back marker, wrap and turn.

Row 6: Work in St st to 18 sts on opposite side of center-back marker, wrap and turn.

Work in the Round

Knit 1 rnd.

BO 6 sts at center front and 6 sts at center back—68 (80, 92, 100) sts.

Legs

Place half of rem sts on dpns for first leg—34 (40, 46, 50) sts. Pm and join. Place rem sts on holder for second leg.

Work even in patt until piece measures 6¼ (7¾, 9¾, 11)" from BO.

Next rnd: Knit, dec 16 (18, 22, 24) sts evenly around—18 (22, 24, 26) sts.

Work in garter st for 2 (2¼, 2¾, 3)". BO 9 (11, 12, 13) sts at front of leg. Change to E and work even in garter st, inc 1 st at each end of next row—11 (13, 14, 15) sts. Work even until piece measures 2¼ (2¾, 3, 3½)" from BO. BO. Fold up "pocket" for foot and sew in place.

Rep for other leg.

Sleeves

Place 22 (26, 29, 31) held sleeve sts on dpns. Join yarn and CO 6 sts at underarm—28 (32, 35, 37) sts. Pm to mark beg of rnd.

Work even in St st for 4¼ (5½, 6¾, 7¾)".

Next (dec) rnd: Knit, dec 8 (8, 11, 13) sts evenly around—20 (24, 24, 24) sts.

Work even in garter st for 2 (2, 2¼, 2¼)".

Next rnd: K5 (6, 6, 6), BO 10 (12, 12, 12) sts, K5 (6, 6, 6).

Change to E and work even in garter st, inc 1 st at each end of next row—12 (14, 14, 14) sts.

Work even until piece measures 2¼ (2¼, 2¾, 2¾)" from BO. BO. Fold up "pocket" for hand and sew in place.

Rep for other sleeve.

Finishing

Weave in ends. Block. Sew buttons opposite buttonholes.

Winter Baby Hat and Mittens

Winter babies need warm and cute clothes. Here's a set with hat and mitts to make Baby's first months cozy.

SKILL LEVEL: Easy

Sizes

To fit ages 0–3 (3–6) months

HAT

Circumference: 12¼ (14½)"

MITTENS

Circumference: 4½ (4½)"

Materials

DK-weight merino wool (100% merino wool; 50 g; 153 yds) in the following amounts and colors: ③

A: 153 (153) yds in gray

B: 153 (153) yds in red

C: 153 (153) yds in cream

D: 153 (153) yds in peach

US Size 4 (3.5 mm) 16" circular and double-pointed needles, or size needed to obtain gauge

Stitch markers, stitch holders, tapestry needle

Gauge

21½ sts and = 4" in St st

Hat

With circular needle and A, CO 66 (78) sts. Pm and join, being careful not to twist the sts. Work in K1, P1 rib for 1 (1½)".

Note: Earflaps are worked by increasing in each st over the ears, then separating out every other st to make 2 layers of fabric, which are knit separately.

Next rnd: Work 5 (6) sts in patt, pm, K1f&b over next 15 (18) sts, pm, work next 26 (30) sts in patt, pm, K1f&b over next 15 (18) sts, pm, work in patt to end—96 (114) sts.

Next rnd: *Work in patt to first marker, place every other st on holder and hold to back to next marker for earflap; rep from * for last 2 markers and second earflap, work in patt to end—66 (78) sts.

Change to St st. Work even, changing colors as desired in stripe patt, until piece measures 4 (5)".

Shape Crown

Change to dpns when needed.

Rnd 1: *K4, K2tog; rep from * around—55 (65) sts.

Rnds 2, 4, 6, and 8: Knit.

Rnd 3: *K3, K2tog; rep from * around—44 (52) sts.

Rnd 5: *K2, K2tog; rep from * around—33 (39) sts.

Rnd 7: *K1, K2tog; rep from * around—22 (26) sts.

Rnd 9: *K2tog; rep from * around—11 (13) sts.

Cut yarn, draw through rem sts, pull tight, and secure.

Earflaps

Place 15 (18) held sts on needles. With A, work in garter st (knit every row) and dec 1 st each end of row every other row until 3 sts rem. Work even over rem 3 sts until tie is desired length. BO. Rep on other earflap.

Finishing

Weave in ends. Block.

Mittens

With dpns and A, CO 24 (24) sts. Pm and join, being careful not to twist the sts. Work in K1, P1 rib for 1½ (2)". Work in patt as follows:

Rnd 1: *K1, P1; rep from * around.

Rnd 2: *K1, K1b; rep from * around.

Rnd 3: *P1, K1; rep from * around.

Rnd 4: *K1b, K1; rep from * around.

Rep rnds 1–4 until piece measures 3½ (4½)", ending with rnd 4.

Shape Top

Rnd 1: *K3tog, P1; rep from * around—18 (18) sts.

Rnd 2: *K1, K1b; rep from * around.

Rnd 3: *P1, K2tog; rep from * around—12 (12) sts.

Rnd 4: *K1b, K1; rep from * around.

Cut yarn, draw through rem sts, pull tight, and secure.

Finishing

Weave in ends. Block.

. . . .

Plain Vest

Knit this super-simple pattern for a boy or a girl. For girls you can even knit it a bit longer to make it a tunic to wear over tights. It has a '70s shape, but if you'd like it to have a bit more hold at the bottom, cast on eight fewer stitches at the start and increase eight stitches during the first round of Stockinette stitch.

SKILL LEVEL: EASY

Gauge

13 sts and 20 rows = 4" in St st with 1 strand of each yarn held tog

Body

Hold 1 strand of each yarn tog throughout.

CO 72 (80, 88, 94, 102, 108) sts. Pm and join, being careful not to twist sts.

Work in garter st (knit 1 rnd, purl 1 rnd) for 16 rnds.

Pm 36 (40, 44, 47, 51, 54) sts from first marker to mark opposite side "seam." Work even in St st until piece measures 6¾ (7, 8¾, 9½, 8¾, 10½)".

Beg working garter st edging for underarms as follows:

Rnd 1: P6, knit to 6 sts before marker, sl marker, P6, knit to last 6 sts, P6—12 garter sts on each side.

Rnd 2: Knit.

Rep rnds 1 and 2 two more times.

Sizes

To fit ages 1 (2, 3–4, 5–6, 7–8, 9–10) years

Chest: 22 (24½, 27, 29, 31½, 33¼)"

Length: 12¼ (13, 15, 16, 17¾, 19½)"

Materials

196 (294, 392, 392, 392, 490 yds) of DK-weight cotton (100% cotton; 50 g; 98 yds) in rust **3**

209 (418, 418, 418, 418, 627 yds) of fingering-weight alpaca (100% alpaca; 50 g; 209 yds) in rust **1**

US Size 9 (5.5 mm) 24" circular needle, or size needed to obtain gauge

Next rnd: BO 2 sts, knit to 2 sts before marker, BO 4 sts (remove marker), knit to last 2 sts, BO 2 sts—32 (36, 40, 43, 47, 50) sts each on front and back. Place back sts on holder and continue in rows on 32 (36, 40, 43, 47, 50) front sts only.

Front

Work in St st, keeping first and last 4 sts in garter st, until piece measures 10¼ (11, 12¾, 13¾, 15, 16)". Knit 6 rows.

Next row (RS): K9 (11, 12, 13, 14, 15) sts, join a second ball of yarn and loosely BO center 14 (14, 16, 17, 19, 20) sts, knit to end.

Working each side separately at the same time, knit 8 (8, 10, 12, 12, 12) rows more. Do not BO. Place sts on holders.

Back

Place held sts on needles. Work as for front until piece measures 10¼ (11, 12¾, 13¾, 15, 16)". Work in garter st (knit every row) until piece measures same as front, ending with a WS row.

Next row (RS): K9 (11, 12, 13, 14, 15) sts, join a second ball of yarn and loosely BO center 14 (14, 16, 17, 19, 20) sts, knit to end. Do not BO.

Finishing

Join shoulders using Kitchener st (page 107).

Weave in ends. Block.

. . . .

Knitting Basics

Most of the patterns in this book require basic knitting skills—how to knit and purl, make increases and decreases, how to join new balls of yarn—and so on. Below, you'll find information of the techniques we use in case you are unfamiliar with any of them.

Basic Stitches

Knit. Knit stitches are worked one at a time, inserting the right-hand needle into the first stitch on the left-hand needle, from the left side of the stitch through to behind the left needle. Wrap the working yarn around the right needle, and pull the needle and yarn loop through the stitch on the left needle. Drop the stitch off the left needle. You have knit one stitch onto the right needle.

Purl. Purl stitches are the exact opposite of knit stiches. Purled stitches form a bump or horizontal bar across the front of the work, while knit stitches form a V. If you turn your work over, you'll see that the purled stitch makes a V on the back, while knit stitches have the bar on the back. To work a purl stitch, insert the right-hand needle into the first stitch on the left-hand needle, from right to left in front of the left needle. Wrap the yarn around the right needle and pull the loop through the stitch on the left needle. Drop the stitch off the left needle. You have one purled stitch on the right needle.

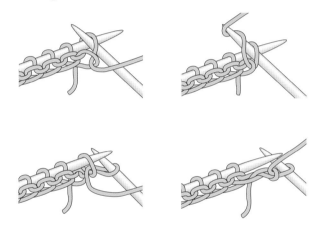

Garter stitch. Garter stitch is the most basic of all knitting; you simply knit all stitches, on both the right and wrong side of the work. It makes a pebbled-feeling fabric.

Stockinette stitch. Stockinette stitch uses both knit and purl stitches. All stitches on the right side are knit, while all stitches on the wrong side are purled. This makes a smooth fabric of V-shaped stitches on the front and bumpy purled stitches on the back.

Garter stitch

Stockinette stitch

Slip stitch. The slip stitch is used primarily to form some sort of decorative knitting effect. By slipping a stitch without knitting it, you are elongating the stitch to stretch from one row to the next. Often used in colorwork to carry one color into the next row of contrasting color to form a pattern, the slip stitch can also be used simple to make longer stitches, such as in the traditional fisherman's rib pattern used to make the Bubble Tunic on page 60.

To work a slip stitch, simply insert the right-hand needle into the next stitch on the left-hand needle and slip the stitch from the left to the right needle without knitting or purling the stitch. If the instructions don't specify which way to slip the stitch, slip it purlwise.

Knit in the row below. Often used in conjunction with a slip stitch, such as to form the fisherman's rib pattern, knitting into the row below is just how it sounds. Instead of knitting into the next stitch on the needle, knit into the stitch directly below the next stitch on the needle. Then slip the stitch above off of the needle.

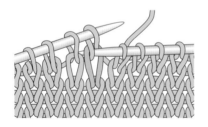

Decreasing, Increasing, and Shaping

While most of the garments in this book are quite easy, sometimes a bit of shaping is needed to form armholes or sleeve openings or the crown of a hat. We use basic increases and decreases, but occasionally also use short rows to shape a piece. Each technique is described and shown below.

Knit 2 together. K2tog is shorthand for "knit two stitches together," or in other words, decreasing one stitch. This is the most commonly used decrease, although it slants to the right so you'll want to pair it with a left-slanting decrease when working a garment with decreases on each side, such as to shape armholes.

To work, insert the right-hand needle into the first two stitches on the left-hand needle, from left to right. That means, you'll insert your needle through the second stitch first, then through the first stitch, then complete the knit stitch as usual. After pulling the yarn loop through both the stitches, slip them off the left needle. You'll have one new stitch on the right needle in place of the two stitches you've slipped off the left needle. One stitch has been decreased.

Slip, slip, knit. This is also a decrease stitch, abbreviated as "ssk," but it slants to the left, or in the opposite direction of K2tog. To make an ssk, insert the right needle into the first stitch on the left needle. Slip it off the left needle and onto the right needle, as if you're knitting (but don't work the stitch). Repeat, slipping a second stitch off the left needle. Now slip the tip of the left needle into the front of the two slipped stitches. (That means the right needle tip will be behind the left needle tip.) Now, wrap the working yarn around the tip of the right needle, pull the loop through both stitches, and slip them off the needles.

Yarn over. A yarn over, abbreviated YO, is a way to increase stitch count. Rather than knitting or purling into another stitch, you simply wrap the yarn around your needle before working the next stitch in the pattern. This loop around the needle will make one more stitch to knit on the following row. But because it wasn't worked into a stitch, this loop also makes a little gap or hole. It's an easy increase, but is generally reserved for patterns where you need a lacy open look or decorative edging.

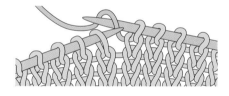

Make 1. The least visible type of increase is to make one left or make one right, abbreviated as M1L or M1R. Like their decrease counterparts, K2tog and ssk, these increases slant to the left and right, letting you shape your garment neatly and symmetrically.

To make one left, insert the left-hand needle under the bar or running thread between the stitch just worked and the next stitch on the left-hand needle, from front to back. Then knit into the back of the stitch as shown, and work this bar as if it were an actual

stitch. Slip the new stitch onto the right-hand needle and continue working the remaining stitches.

Make 1 knitwise: Left cross

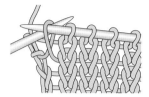 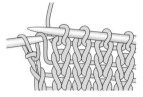

Insert left needle from front to back through "running thread."   Knit into back of stitch.

To make one right, insert the left-hand needle under the bar or running thread between the stitch just worked and the next stitch on the left-hand needle, from back to front. Then knit into the front of the stitch as shown, and work this bar as if it were an actual stitch. Slip the new stitch onto the right-hand needle and continue working the remaining stitches.

Make 1: Right cross

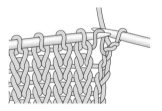 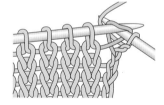

Insert left needle from back to front through "running thread."   Knit into front of stitch.

Backward-loop cast on. Sometimes you'll need to add more than one stitch per row to your knitting, such as when you want to add on some stitches to the sides of a sweater to make sleeves that are joined to the body, rather than added on later. To do this, we use the easiest method—the backward-loop cast on. With this method, you can add on stitches at the beginning of a row, or even in the middle.

To make a backward loop, make a loop with the working yarn that looks like a lowercase "e" and slip the right-hand needle through the loop, as shown below. You can make one or multiple loops; just try to keep the loops loose or as you go to knit them on the following row, your cast-on section will be a bit tight.

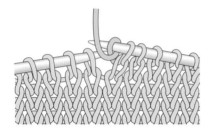

Shaping

Many of the sweaters in this book are designed to have minimal finishing work to assemble them. But that can require some shaping take place to make that possible. For example, one way to avoid having to sew in sleeves is to simply pick up stitches along an edge so you can work the sleeve shaping and have the sleeve attached all at once.

Another way to create shaping is to work short rows. Working short rows allows you to add extra volume or curved shaping to a section of knitting without making standard increases or decreases. Have a look at the Cool Kid Capris on page 12. This pattern uses short-row shaping around the seat of the pants to add volume where it's needed, rather than just increasing stitches along the sides of the garment.

Pick up and knit. Abbreviated as PU, this really stands for "pick up and knit." Generally this type of

picking up stitches is done along the selvage, cast-on, or bound-off edge of a garment, but is also done along the gusset in sock knitting.

To pick up and knit, you'll insert your right-hand needle through the edge of the knitting where instructed, wrap the new working yarn around the needle, and pull the yarn through to make a new stitch on the needle. Continue along in this manner until you've picked up the required number of stitches as specified in the pattern you're knitting.

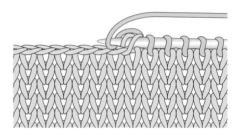

Along bound-off edge

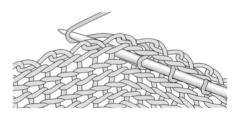

Along rows of knitting

Short rows. Short-row shaping involves knitting a partial row (a short row), turning the work and knitting or purling back as instructed. You may work short on both ends of the row, or just one end, depending on the desired result. This technique lets you build fullness into a pattern to account for curved or rounded body parts. Short rows are worked in two parts—the first row where you make the turn, and the following row where you need to close the gap caused by turning in the middle of a row.

When working short rows, we knit or purl the number of stitches indicated up to the point where we need to turn. Then we wrap the yarn around the stitch when turning, as follows.

Wrap on a knit stitch: Carry the working yarn to the front of the work and slip the next stitch knitwise, carry the yarn to the back again and slip the stitch back onto the left needle without twisting it. You may sometimes see this abbreviated as "W&T" for "wrap and turn."

Slip stitch as if to purl. Move yarn to front of work and slip stitch back to left needle.

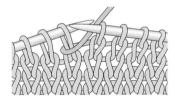

Move yarn to back of work. Turn.

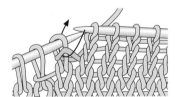

On the final row, knit bar (wrap) and stitch together.

Wrap on a purl stitch: Slip the next stitch purlwise, carry the yarn to the font of the work and slip the stitch back onto the left needle.

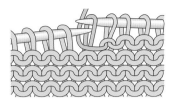

Slip stitch as if to purl. Move yarn to back of work and slip stitch back to left needle.

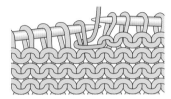

Move yarn toward you. Turn.

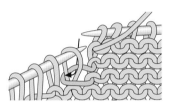

On final row, purl bar (wrap) and stitch together.

Pick up the wrap around a knit stitch: When reaching the stitch with the wrap, put your needle down into the front of the loop that lies around the foot of the stitch, lift it up and slide it onto the left needle without twisting it. K2tog through the back loop.

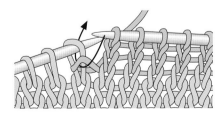

Pick up the wrap around a purl stitch: When reaching the stitch with the wrap, put your needle down into the back of the work on the loop that lies around the foot of the stitch, lift it up and slide it onto the left needle without twisting it. P2tog.

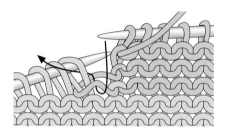

Two-Colored Knitting

Some of the projects in this book use two or more colors to make stripes or more intricate colorwork patterns. Stripes require just one yarn in any given row. The only tricky situation is at the beginning/end of the round. We have a tip for that! For other colorwork patterns, you will need to carry an alternate color along with the main color so that you can change back and forth as needed. This is sometimes referred to as "Fair Isle" knitting or "stranded" knitting.

Stripes. When knitting in the round, the spot where the round ends and the new round begins makes a jog up one row higher. (See photo on page 107.) This is not really noticeable when using just one color of yarn. But when knitting stripes, the colors will make a noticeable jog as you shift from one round to the next. To make a smoother transition, try this trick: Knit one round with the new color. At the beginning of the next round (when you reach the first stitch knit in that new color), knit in the stitch below the first stitch on the left-hand needle. (See "Knit in the row below" on page 102.) This isn't a perfect solution, but making this minor adjustment will make the shift in colors much less

noticeable. From this point on, just continue knitting in the new color until it's time for the next stripe. Each time you change stripe colors, repeat this little trick.

Stranded knitting. When knitting with two or more colors, you'll need to carry the color not being used at the time along the back of your work. This strand is called a "float." The most important thing to remember is to make sure your floats have just the right amount of yarn If you work too tightly there will be no stretch in the garment and it will look as if someone has pulled it together. In the end, the hat or sweater won't fit. If you work too loosely the stitches may start to loosen, especially if you only knit one stitch in one of the colors.

Whenever we change colors, we stretch out the stitches on the right needle, and then carry the yarn behind the work as we use the new color. Check your work periodically to make sure your floats aren't too tight or hanging loosely. The floats should take up the same amount of space as the knitted stitches they're floating behind, as shown in the photo below right.

Finishing

While we try to minimize finishing steps, sometimes they just can't be avoided! So for the times when you need to join openings together seamlessly, we use Kitchener stitch. Here's how to do that, as well as how to make I-cord for ties.

Kitchener stitch. Also known as grafting, this stitch is sewn by hand using a tapestry needle and the working yarn to join two pieces of knitting, or to close up an open end of knitting in the round, such as on socks or booties, to make a smooth join that looks just like the rest of your knitting.

With pieces held wrong sides together (right sides facing out) and the yarn tail at the right end of the needles, work as follows.

1. Weave the yarn through the first stitch on the front needle knitwise and push the stitch off the knitting needle. Then weave the yarn through the next stitch on the front needle purlwise (this is now the first stitch), but leave the stitch on the knitting needle. Gently pull the yarn to match the tension of the rest of the knitted fabric.

2. Weave the yarn purlwise through the first stitch on the back needle and push the yarn off the knitting needle. Again, pull the yarn gently to keep the tension even as the seam closes. Then weave the yarn through the next stitch on the back needle knitwise, but leave it on the knitting needle.

Notice how the bottom orange stripe makes a jog at the start of a new round. The top stripe makes a smoother transition by knitting in the stitch below.

Carry the unused yarn loosely along the wrong side for knitting that lies smooth and flat and doesn't pull too tight.

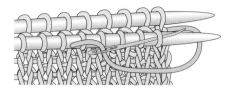

Take the first stitch off
the needle as if to knit.

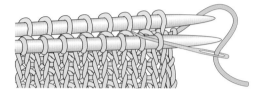

Insert in next stitch as if to purl.
Leave stitch on needle.

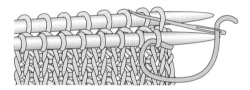

Take the first stitch off the
back needle as if to purl.

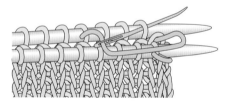

Insert in next stitch as if to knit.
Leave stitch on needle.

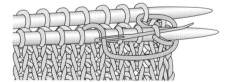

Take the stitch off the
front needle as if to knit.

3. Weave the yarn through the first stitch on the front needles knitwise and push that stitch off the needle. Weave the yarn through the next stitch (now the first stitch) on the front needle purlwise and leave it on the needle.

4. Weave the yarn through the first stitch on the back needle purlwise and push the stitch off the needle. Weave the yarn the next stitch (now the first stitch) on the back needle knitwise and leave it on the needle.

5. Repeat steps 3 and 4 until there are two stitches left, one in front and one in back. Weave the yarn through the first stitch on the needle knitwise, and then push that stitch off the needle. Weave the yarn through the first stitch on the back needle purlwise and push it off the needle. Pull the tapestry needle and yarn through to the wrong side and weave in the tail.

Here's the shorthand mantra to repeat to yourself as you graft your stitching.

Begin with:

Front knit off, purl on

Back purl off, knit on

Continue with:

Front knit off, purl on

Back purl off, knit on

End with:

Front knit off

Back purl off

I-cord. I-cord is a quick and easy way to make a knitted cord that can be used as a drawstring for pants as well as for ties on a hat or a cord to keep two mittens together. I-cord is worked on two double-pointed needles or a circular needle. The right side of the cord will always be facing you as you knit.

Cast on the number of stitches called for in the project instructions. Knit one row, but DO NOT turn the work. *Slide all the stitches to the opposite end of the needle. The working yarn is now at the end of the needle away from the tip where you will start knitting. Pull the working yarn snugly behind the stitches to the tip and knit across all the stitches. Repeat from * until your I-cord measures the desired length. Bind off. Give the cord a little tug to even out all the stitches and then notice how you now have a cord that is knit in the round.

Unattached I-cord

Abbreviations

beg   begin(ning)

BO   bind off

ch(s)   chain(s)

CO   cast on

cont   continue(ing)

dec(s)   decrease(s)

dpn(s)   double-pointed needle(s)

g   grams

inc(s)   increase(s)(ing)

K1b   knit 1 in stitch of row below

K1f&b   knit into front and back of same st—1 stitch increased

K2tog   knit 2 stitches together—1 stitch decreased

K3tog   knit 3 stitches together—2 stitches decreased

kw   knitwise

LH   left hand

M1   make 1 stitch

M1L   make 1 left (from the front, lift strand between stitches with left needle, knit into back of loop)

M1LP   make 1 left purl

M1R   make 1 right (from the back, lift strand between stitches with left needle, knit into front of loop)

M1RP   make 1 right purl

oz   ounces

P   purl

P1b   purl 1 in stitch of row below

patt(s)   pattern(s)

pm   place marker

psso   pass slipped stitch over

P2tog   purl 2 together—1 stitch decreased

PU   pick up and knit

rem   remain(ing)

rev   reverse

RH   right hand

RS   right side

sc   single crochet

sl   slip

sl 1   slip 1 stitch

tbl   through back loop(s)

ssk   slip, slip, knit 3 stitches together—2 stitches decreased

st(s)   stitch(es)

St st   Stockinette stitch (knit 1 row, purl 1 row; knit every row in the round)

tog   together

wfib   with yarn in back

wyif   with yarn in front

WS   wrong side

yd(s)   yard(s)

YO   yarn over

Useful Information

Standard Yarn-Weight System

Yarn-Weight Symbol and Category Name	**1** Super Fine	**2** Fine	**3** Light	**4** Medium	**5** Bulky	**6** Super Bulky
Types of Yarn in Category	Sock, Fingering, Baby	Sport, Baby	DK, Light Worsted	Worsted, Afghan, Aran	Chunky, Craft, Rug	Bulky, Roving
Knit Gauge Range* in Stockinette Stitch to 4"	27 to 32 sts	23 to 26 sts	21 to 24 sts	16 to 20 sts	12 to 15 sts	6 to 11 sts
Recommended Needle in US Size Range	1 to 3	3 to 5	5 to 7	7 to 9	9 to 11	11 and larger
Recommended Needle in Metric Size Range	2.25 to 3.25 mm	3.25 to 3.75 mm	3.75 to 4.5 mm	4.5 to 5.5 mm	5.5 to 8 mm	8 mm and larger

These are guidelines only. The above reflect the most commonly used gauges and needle sizes for specific yarn categories.

Metric Conversion

Yards	=	meters	x	1.09
Meters	=	yards	x	0.9144
Ounces	=	grams	x	0.035
Grams	=	ounces	x	28.35

About the Authors

Heidi (left) and Anna

ANNA ENGE and HEIDI GRØNVOLD are knitwear designers and yarn shop owners working from Norway, Scandinavia. The design duo's work has been featured in numerous national and international knitting and home-interior magazines and websites, including knitsy.com, apartmenttherapy.com, craftzine.com, elledecoration.se, and molliemakes.com.

Their blog, www.pickles.no, has thousands of visitors every day and is a source of inspiration for knitters all over the world. Anna and Heidi are often invited to teach workshops as well as show their work and yarns at international and national knitting festivals.

Among their customers, Anna and Heidi are known for playing with color and designing patterns with seam-free construction. Many of their designs are perfect for beginners or people that have not knit for a while. Their favorite wools to work with are from their own Pickles yarn line, and they only stock yarns they love. Anna and Heidi work with small producers from all over the world to carefully select color palettes to achieve a quality result. Anna and Heidi first met working as Art Directors at a large advertising agency in Oslo. Both have a background in art and have been knitting since they were kids, learning the craft in school as most Norwegian children do. After meeting at work, Anna and Heidi founded the Pickles pattern blog that started it all. When it comes to their knitwear designs, they like to avoid mainstream palettes and colors, instead using their art backgrounds to select unusual colors and fibers.

Sweet Pickles is their first book in English.